the book of

meditation

Practical Ways to Health and Healing

Chris Jarmey

JOURNEY EDITIONS

Boston • Tokyo • Singapore

First published by Element, a division of HarperCollins*Publishers*

This edition first published in 2001 by Journey Editions, an imprint of Tuttle Publishing and Periplus Editions (HK) Ltd., with editorial offices at 153 Milk Street, Boston, Massachusetts 02109.

Library of Congress Cataloging-in-Publication Data in process

ISBN: 1-58290-059-0

Distributed in the United States by

Tuttle Publishing
Distribution Center
Airport Industrial Park
364 Innovation Drive
North Clarendon, VT 05759-9436
Tel: (802) 773-8930
Tel: (800) 526-2778
Fax: (802) 773-6993

First edition
06 05 04 03 02 01   10 9 8 7 6 5 4 3 2 1

Studio photography by Guy Hearn
Text illustrations by Jane Spencer
Calligraphy by Joan Corlass

Printed and bound in Singapore

The Author

Chris Jarmey has had a keen interest in yoga and meditation since the age of nine. Since then he has practiced many forms of meditation within several meditation systems, largely through his interest in consciousness, eastern philosophies and his work as a leading teacher of bodywork and oriental medicine. Chris lived in various yoga centers for many years and has since spent large periods of time practicing meditation in Buddhist centers, as well as researching its application and benefits through his work. Throughout this time he has also studied Daoist meditation methods extensively. He is grateful to have received guidance in these profound arts from many eminent teachers.

Acknowledgements

Many people have influenced me in regard to meditation throughout the years. In particular I wish to acknowledge: Ven. Geshe Damcho Yonten and all the residents of Lam Rim Buddhist Center; staff at the FPMT Buddhist Center at Osel Ling; Mother Sayama, Saya U Chit Tin and staff at the International Meditation Centers; Swamis Vishnu Devananda, Chidananda, Satyananda and Satchidananda, who were all disciples of H.H. Sri Swami Sivananda Maharaj.

I would also like to convey my gratitude to all those who gave constructive feedback on the text, namely: Susan Millington PhD, Margaret Travis of Lam Rim Buddhist Center, Liz Welch and George Dellar. Special thanks to my wife Debbie, who not only painstakingly read through the text, giving constructive comments, but who kept family and household in order while I more or less abandoned them during the writing of this book.

Thanks also to Belinda Budge, Nicky Vimpany and other staff at HarperCollins*Publishers*, whose hard work enabled this book to become manifest in your hand.

CONTENTS

Many books on meditation exist, reflecting the rich and diverse spiritual practices and religions that can be found throughout the world. *The Book of Meditation* offers accessible meditation methods and techniques drawn from numerous sources, but especially from the lineages of Buddhism, Indian Yoga, and Daoism. These traditions have a particularly extensive reservoir of detailed instruction on the subject, from sources spanning thousands of years.

In addition to explaining the commonly defined purpose of meditation, which is to enhance one's awareness of 'ultimate reality', this book identifies a variety of other uses that will yield very tangible results, for example meditations and visualizations for the enhancement of health and the management of ill health. Meditations to enhance such things as your will power are included and common obstacles are examined, with solutions suggested for each one.

Another invaluable feature of this book is that it is copiously illustrated, to complement the clear theoretical information and the step-by-step guides to the meditations described.

GENERAL OVERVIEW OF

MEDITATION PRINCIPLES

GOOD REASONS FOR MEDITATING

Many people meditate in order to reap the very tangible benefits that meditation can bring. The main benefits to be gained in the short term will be expanded upon later, but in the meantime they are as follows:

- an enhanced ability to relax
- greater equanimity
- improved self-assurance
- increased physical and mental energy

In addition to these short-term benefits, all forms of meditation gently coax our minds into a greater appreciation of the present moment. This is useful, because relating to the present causes us to be much more focused and alert. When we are not meditating, we spend a surprising amount of time daydreaming about future possibilities or past events. Although reminiscing and planning can be fun and sometimes relaxing, it is good to be in a position to choose when to indulge in fantasy and when to be relating to what is happening now. By giving us the ability to focus at will upon the moment, meditation becomes a tool that enables us to experience things as they actually are.

From time to time we spontaneously experience a lucid connection with the present moment. These times are characterized by the complete melding of our mind with the reality of the present. For example, it is quite likely that you have occasionally experienced the serenity of mind that results from gazing at a beautiful sunset. At such times we suspend our reminiscing about the past, fantasizing about scenarios that are not happening, and the planning or predicting of future things.

Being transfixed with a view of the setting sun can be an unintended meditation for many people. There is also a specific meditation technique centered around this very activity, which is given later. It is also possible for the adrenaline buzz resulting from sudden danger or the thrill of other excitements to put us into this lucid state for short periods of time. But lucidity from excitement reflects a hormonal 'high', which unfortunately must be balanced by an emotional 'low', because life between such stimulation seems very dull by contrast.

The thrill of hormonal highs can be prolonged through the use of various chemicals, but because the body and mind are designed and programed to seek balance, prolonged highs lead to even deeper lows. That path eventually leads to addiction in an attempt to hide from the lows and prolong the highs. We can become addicted to things like drugs, danger, thrills and sex, but nature always seeks to maintain balance. Hence, such addictions, whilst at times providing an almost 'illumined' state of 'awareness', are ultimately paid for by the complete exhaustion of one's hormonal system. In other words, your health and potential for longevity is compromised, and in reality you spend much more time depressed and craving for that 'alive' feeling than actually experiencing it.

So, what goes up must come down. Every front must have a back. As we'll see later, yin must be balanced with yang and yang with yin (see pages 166–168), and so on. I am not saying that excitement is bad, but maybe it would be nice to have that lucid awareness of how things actually are without prematurely exhausting our reserves of vitality, or risking our life, to get it. Meditation offers a more balanced approach, which leads to a more constant state of awareness or 'aliveness'. Better still, it is actually strengthening for your hormonal system, safe to do, and likely to prolong your life expectancy. If you still want to dive out of an aircraft or cling to a rockface by your fingernails, meditation will enable you to do it with even greater insight and awareness, without the downer that normally follows.

Waking up

Basically, what it all boils down to is an understanding of past, present and future. The past has happened, gone forever, and you cannot do anything about it. In addition, your recollection of it is subjective and flawed, insofar as memory is selective. The future is just speculation; it might not even happen at all. That leaves only the present. Now is where reality lives, and you must be here to experience it. You cannot recall it for analysis and you cannot plan to intercept it. All you can do is stop wondering and scheming, pondering and dreaming, and just wake up. This book gives clues to achieving that state of being.

Letting go

Why are we so obsessed with reminiscing, fantasizing and planning? Is it that we want what we have not got? Do we know what we have got? What are we afraid of losing? Will such fear help us keep it anyway?

If we surround ourselves with enough possessions, the assumption is that we will eventually be content. If we can gather sufficient power and fame, we will presumably be secure. Why then is smiling not directly proportional to such states? Or why, according to statistics, do suicides seem to occur with greater frequency amongst the more wealthy and secure?

To live a more meditative life does not mean living without aspirations or without using our initiative. On the contrary, it means living in a state of wakefulness, free from the wasteful grasping for things which we think will make us happy. When properly awake, you can secure what you actually need, acquire what is genuinely useful, and ignore that which is not helpful. For instance, if you need a financial fortune to help out in some

way, then being fully awake and focused will help you obtain it.

Waking up will make clear what is and what is not an obsession. Being awake means seeing the full picture and therefore having the best and most balanced perspective. Hence, there is no judgement of good or bad and right or wrong in relation to your activities in life. It is all down to enhancing your awareness, and acting in accordance with that clarity of perception.

Here are a few questions that spring to mind in relation to grasping:

- Do you want what he or she has got just because you have not got it?
- Would you still want it if the perceived value of it disappeared in the eyes of others?
- How much energy will it take to keep it and protect it?
- Will those who have not got what you have really love you more because you have it?

The point is: there is nothing wrong with having as long as you are prepared to lose it with grace and equanimity. That is easy to agree with until the crunch comes, when you actually do lose it. Then what? Well, the idea is that a strong foundation of meditative practice will help you see things clearly and in true perspective, through both calm and stormy seas, without losing your composure. It will not make losing your home or your close relative a non-event, but it will prevent you from being dragged into a mire of self-pity. It is painful to lose things, especially living things, and it is right and normal to grieve, but being locked in grief does not bring anything back, except obsessive memories which obscure the present. I know it sounds hard, but if you actually think about that, it is quite compassionate, both for the mourners and for those with whom they come into contact. Here's a little saying that might capture the drift of this message:

Mourn the departed for as long as they miss you. Mourn for those who await your release from mourning. Mourn for yourself for as long as it takes to realize the wisdom of this.

The message is clear. We must disentangle ourselves from the unnecessary complexities of life brought on by our grasping, clinging minds. Grasping is what enslaves us. The antidote to grasping is 'letting go'.

Accepting what is

Letting go sounds simple, but it is not easy. On the occasions when one truly stops grasping, reality can come as a bit of a surprise. No longer is it coloured by our judgements and prejudices; it is the raw and honest truth. If the truth seems bad, then you are not yet fully aware of it; you are still holding on to your judgement of it. If it seems good, you are also not seeing it from a panoramic perspective. Reality just is. Good is always in contrast to bad and vice-versa. 'Is' is like the vista from the top of the mountain, where one sees all points of view.

So should we try to change anything? That is an interesting philosophical question. Both sides in a conflict think they are right and believe the other side is wrong. True perspective means we see what is, without prejudice. This more holistic view of life is what we trust will arise out of our meditative perseverance. It is noticeable that true sages do not go around forcing issues, but inspire others to seek a truer perspective. Therefore, if we can be more like the sages, we are more likely to influence things positively by not trying to

change anything. Anyway, until we are firmly established in the reality of the present, that is, 'awakened', who are we to judge anything at all?

Perseverance

What then, will help us to persevere with meditation practice? First, we must be motivated. For that, we need to have a high ethical reason for meditating. For example, we might not have considered getting involved with it had we not observed a greater equanimity and compassion amongst those who are firmly established in it. Therefore, it is a good idea to make sure you cross paths with those people from time to time, or at least remind yourself of those qualities and benefits through clear writings on the subject. Above all, reflect on the benefits meditation brings you when you actually get around to doing it yourself. In addition, keep reminding yourself of the following:

- The less you do it, the more inertia there is to overcome before you can get started. Some self-discipline is therefore required, but regularity of practice will make this easier. Most importantly, do not chastise yourself for not doing it, because guilt is not a strong motivator.
- Remember that everything in the universe operates within cycles. Therefore, highs and lows are natural. Downs must be followed by ups and vice-versa.
- Apparent lack of progress is disheartening, but remember that for all meditators, the meditation process is a case of two steps forward and one step backward (or sometimes two or three steps backward). On balance you will make progress, but yearning for progress takes us out of the present and locks us into imaginings of future things. It is easy to continue when progress seems to be

happening, but hard when it is not. You will need to make a habit of letting go, learn to accept your mindset, and then just do it! If you miss a session, do not punish yourself, but observe with non-judgemental interest that you simply did not do it that day. So try again the next day.

Focusing the mind

What then, should we be focusing on? Any object or subject will do, but the simpler the better, especially in the early stages. As you progress through this book, you will find many examples of suitable subjects and objects.

Those people who do not practice meditation can be forgiven for believing they might be better employed doing something useful and creative instead. However, once you begin to practice meditation (reading about it is useful, but not enough), you will find that your ability to focus your mind is progressively developed. So, rather than suppressing creativity and the imagination, meditation will enhance them.

People might also be forgiven at this stage for wondering what the difference is between the focus of meditation and the focus required for less noble activities. To make the point with an extreme and slightly facetious comparison, let us compare meditation with the act of creeping around a house with a view to burglary. It is true that something like burglary requires total alertness and focus, but there are differences. The concentration of burglary is a state of high tension, easily diverted by any sudden threat of discovery. It is adrenaline based and therefore accompanied by increased heartbeat and nervous tension. It is not motivated by compassion or high ethics, and after the act, burglars are probably totally exhausted. Emotions will be elated if sufficient booty was gathered, or depressed

if it was insufficient. Either way, equanimity of mind will elude the burglar.

Meditation will bring physiological and emotional results exactly opposite to the focus of burglary. The focus of meditation will move us towards patience, clarity, compassion and wisdom, and away from resistance, distractedness, indifference and overreaction.

Obstacles to meditation

Meditation is inherently simple but not easy. The more you do it, the more you will become aware of the things that seem to hinder you. It is not that doing it creates more obstacles, but that doing it makes you more aware of things in general, including the obstacles and resistances you bring to your meditation practice.

The classic obstacles, affectionately called 'hindrances' in meditation terminology, are:

- dullness (sleepiness)
- restlessness (from boredom, pain or an agitated mind)
- negativity (simply the natural balance for over optimism)
- desire (wanting to reject the moment we are in and jump to a better moment)
- doubt (thinking no progress is happening or possible)
- aversion (wanting to be doing something else)

These hindrances will definitely arise, so accept them as inevitable and wait for them to disperse. Later in this book, you will find specific meditation practices to help you accept or let go of these hindrances, should they persist. It is worth remembering, however, that hindrances are not signs of spiritual failure, but opportunities to acquaint us with our mental landscape. They are not enemies but doors into greater levels of insight.

Going back to the above list of hindrances, desire warrants some further explanation. First, desire forces your mind into fantasy mode, because the moment you see or perceive something you want, you will fantasize about what you could do with it, or how it will enhance your pleasure or add to your self-esteem. For example, you might desire extra money. Why? Because you imagine all the things you could buy with it. As a result, your mind is forced into a fantasy about the future, even though you do not yet have that money to fulfill the fantasy.

The other problem with desire is that one fulfilled desire can spawn a hundred more, because desire is inherently insatiable. A story I heard from Swami Vishnu Devananda, which is also quoted in his book *Meditation and Mantras*, illustrates this well:

"There was once a monk who retired to a cave in the Himalayas. He had only two possessions – the loincloth he was wearing and an extra one. Returning one day from a distant village where he had gone to beg for food, he found that the spare loincloth had been chewed by a rat.

He bought another cloth and the same thing happened. So he bought a cat to get rid of the rat. The cat disposed of the rat, but it had to have milk. It is difficult to buy milk in an Indian village, and as daily expeditions for it would have been too time consuming, the monk bought a cow. It is difficult to feed and milk a cow, look after its needs, tend to a cat and pursue intensive spiritual practice. Needing help, the renunciate got married, and everything he had renounced came back to him."

To make progress it is not necessary to be a renunciate, as required of a monk. But it is a question of degree. The message is: the simpler your needs, the easier it is to overcome hindrances and the easier it is to keep your mind in the present.

So, what if you are living a busy life in the material world? Does it mean there is no point in even trying? On the contrary, meditation might be difficult at first, but it will gradually disentangle your thought patterns, help you identify the trivial and offer a clear perspective on life.

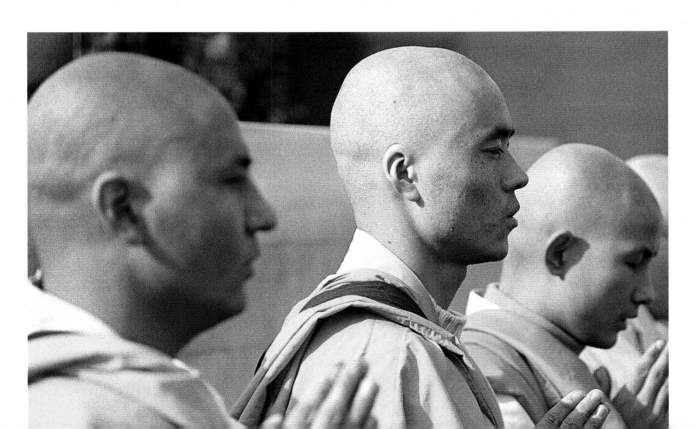

DEFINING MINDFULNESS

To practice mindfulness means to be constantly aware or conscious of everything we do. It requires us to keep our minds absorbed in the present moment, noticing the details and nuances of our actions. For example, if we wash a cup with mindfulness, we notice the texture and temperature of the cup. We are aware of how much pressure we are applying to the cup with the cloth or brush. We take note of the speed with which we are conducting the activity, and we become aware of our own physical sensations and thought processes. It certainly prevents us from rushing.

The more repetitive or routine the activity, the more likely it is that we will switch to autopilot and allow our minds to dwell elsewhere. This is certainly necessary, to provide us with time to make plans or to reminisce. But in our busy, complicated lives we perhaps spend too much time pondering the trivial, dwelling on the past or anticipating future possibilities. We tend to miss a full appreciation of the present, because our minds are perpetually oscillating backwards and forwards through time and space. The past is history and the future is only a possibility – it might not even happen. The only 'reality' for us is what our consciousness perceives right now.

So, if you wash that cup with your full attention, you will learn a great deal about that cup.

If you are a healer applying a healing touch with your full attention, you will learn a lot about your touch and about how your touch is received. If you make mindfulness a priority and a discipline, you will spend much more time in the here and now. Consequently, you will learn a lot about yourself and about how you interact with others. Your healing touch will naturally become more sensitive, more empathic, and thus, more effective.

Mindfulness develops sensitivity to what is going on within you. As a result it develops equanimity, because equanimity is the opposite of succumbing to distractions. To illustrate the relevance of this, imagine you are the receiver of some form of healing treatment. In that situation, you will definitely feel more at ease when worked on by a serene and centred person, compared to being treated by someone who is clearly preoccupied with some other issue: the former will feel great and the latter will hurt or irritate you.

One of the easiest ways to practice mindfulness is to observe your own breathing. As long as you are alive you will be breathing, so if breath is the object of your attention, you know you cannot forget to bring it with you. A good technique is to observe the breath as it enters and leaves your nostrils, trying to notice any sensations felt at the point of entry and exit. You may feel this close to the tip of your nose, just inside the nostrils or between your nose and your top lip. Experiment to see which applies to you. Try to register only those sensations felt at this point; in other words, do not follow the breath deeper into the body on the inhalation, or

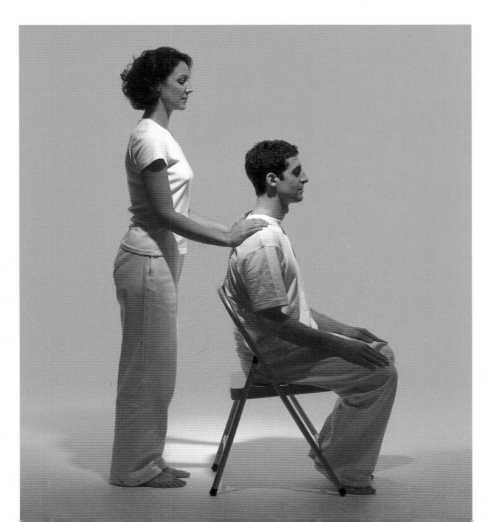

beyond the nose on the exhalation. Like a toll booth operator, you are simply checking the passage of traffic as it actually passes back and forth through the gate.

Alternatively, you could be aware of your belly moving slightly in and out as you breathe, relating only to the sensation of your lower belly 'opening' a little as you inhale and 'closing' a little as you exhale. Again, avoid following the breath to see where it goes (although you could do that once or twice as a separate meditation, just to find out). These techniques are examples of a mindfulness of breath method known as anapana.

If you practice breathing with awareness, you will remember to do other things with more awareness. Try not to get obsessive about it though, or broadcast the fact that you are doing it, because it is not helpful to draw unnecessary attention to this activity. Just quietly continue until it becomes a natural and unobtrusive part of your way of being. You will be pleasantly surprised by the fringe benefits, particuarly the way in which you are able to cope with your own stress more positively.

Mindfulness requires a sort of detached concentration.

However, when firmly established as a practice, mindfulness yields a different quality from concentration in that concentration excludes things that are not the object of concentration, whereas mindfulness includes the spectrum of all things within your perception at any given moment. Mindfulness gives us the qualities of:

■ **Sensitivity**
Nothing is judged to be unworthy of our attention. Thus, everything that comes into our perception is greeted equally.

■ **Oneness**
Our heart, body and mind become more integrated, making us receptive to all things without judgement, rather than emotionally reactive to them.

■ **Clarity**
Mindfulness is like a mirror, simply reflecting without preference what is actually happening in each moment. It dissolves the habit of judging and reacting, and leads to clarity of perception, which results in greater calmness.

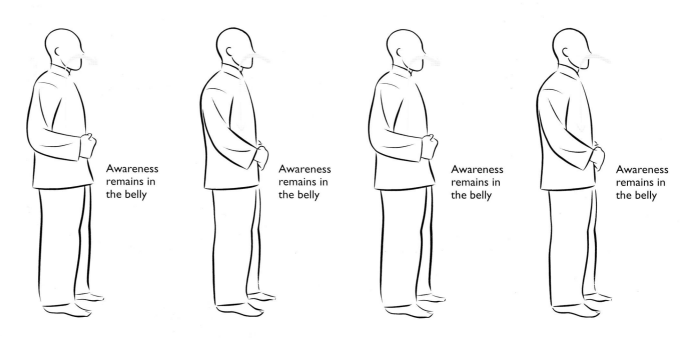

Awareness remains in the belly

Awareness remains in the belly

Awareness remains in the belly

Awareness remains in the belly

When the mind is not mindful and attentive, it follows its habitual patterns of liking, disliking, rejecting, pursuing, projecting, and being for and against things. Clear attentiveness is awareness that is free from the process of reacting, without adding or subtracting anything from the experience. Confusion dissipates and clarity and equanimity emerge.

Mindfulness is distinguished from the concentration of the juggler or athlete by the intention to awaken and transform, and to nurture an understanding of the true nature of experience. Mindfulness does not foster new theories or belief systems, but simply focuses our mind upon the essential clarity and reality of our own experiences. It causes us to awaken and free ourselves from pondering what might have been or what could be.

Mindfulness of body

Exploring our relationship to pain and pleasure within our bodies helps us to gain insight into that relationship, both at the physical and emotional levels. Our natural tendency is to flee from the unpleasant because we have learned to fear it, avoid it and suppress it, thus ending up living a life of anxiety and struggle.

With practice, if we observe pain and pleasure rather than indulge it, different levels of sensation will emerge, which we can eventually learn to relinquish. In this way, there will be a release of superficial tensions, and, eventually, of any deeply buried pain created through past emotional or psychological trauma. However, it is not just pain and trauma that come to the surface. We will also see compassion, generosity and love increasingly arise within us. Just as well, because if all we got was pain and aggravation, we would soon give up!

Mindfulness and anapana (concentration on the breath) are examples of meditation. However, meditation encompasses any method that helps to counteract the wandering tendency of our mind so that we can experience things as they really are. It is the term given to those practices that encourage a genuinely objective view of things. Our mistaken view of reality is that we relate to things as if they have some permanent existence, inherently independent of other things.

We think of a 10,000-year-old stone statue as a stone statue, forgetting that it is only a rock hewn from another rock, and that it will eventually be eroded into dust. We know this if we are drawn to think about it, but most of the time we do not think this way. We slip into our habit of perceiving such things as absolute unchanging objects. Likewise, we see a person as attractive, or we experience ice cream as delicious. But surely, if these qualities were inherent within those things, everyone would experience them in the same way, which of course they do not. The well-known saying "beauty is in the eye of the beholder" illustrates this concept well.

The ongoing awareness that things are both forever changing and ultimately interlinked with all other things is the 'reality' that eludes us. We experience fleeting moments of awakening, but when it really matters, we fall back into our habitually limited way of perceiving things. We can take our own experiences as examples: when someone annoys us, we react angrily because they are annoying us, much more so than we would if they were annoying some-body else. And is it really that annoying anyway? Think how much more pleasant it would be if we could maintain a broader overview of our actions and reactions towards others.

Now, as you get slightly annoyed with me and imme-diately say to yourself "I would never react like that," admit to yourself that you have reacted like that and know that we can all only benefit from a consistently more objective and 'present' mind.

Some benefits of meditation

The ultimate goal of the full-time meditator is to remain in a state of 'reality awareness' long enough to perceive what life and the universe is all about. However, for full-time and part-time meditators, the short-term benefits consist of:

- greater equilibrium and clarity of mind, naturally leading to greater patience and tolerance of others
- less stress, because seemingly stressful things are seen in perspective and therefore provoke a more positive reaction
- better health, because positive mental attitudes can help to heal physical and emotional problems
- fewer unrealistic expectations of people or things, therefore less disappointments and better relationships
- more realistic and positive self-image as our per-ception of reality broadens and deepens

Empathy and compassion

In addition to sharpening your mental focus, it is also important to become less self-centered and more caring towards others. If your motivation in life genuinely is to help others, then of course you will have this quality already. Making a habit of reflecting deeply about the needs and suffering of others will enhance your caring attitude. Please remember that a focused mind does not necessarily mean a compassionate mind. One can focus one's selfishness and hate as easily (if not more easily) than one can focus compassion. You need compassion to develop empathy, and you need empathy to enhance compassion.

So, why might we want to meditate? Answer: to con-nect with reality and therefore realize the interconnect-edness of all things. To realize interconnectedness or unity, you need to surrender your belief in separateness. You must constantly remember that every person and creature is interdependent at many levels. Meditation and mindfulness will help you do that.

Stabilizing and analytical meditation

There are two broad categories of meditation: stabilizing meditation and analytical meditation, each of which consists of many methods.

Stabilizing meditations are basically concentration exercises designed to settle the mind into a period of uninterrupted focus on a single point – this is the exact opposite of our usual state of mind, which is forever dis-tracted. Practicing mindfulness and concentrating on the breath, both described earlier, are examples of this. Concentrating on a visualized image, a concept, or a mantra are other examples.

Analytical meditations, on the other hand, involve periods when you consciously draw your mind to reflect upon and analyze a particular concept such as 'emptiness,' 'attachment,' or the nature of mind itself. The purpose of this method is to gain a conceptual understanding of how things are, to a depth that gives you enough clarity to convince you of the true nature of that concept. The process initially involves identifying wrong conceptions. For example, if you are exploring compassion, you would aim to arrive at some insight about compassion by first eliminating your misconceptions about compassion. Analytical meditation is therefore an intensive period of inward study. As such, analytical meditation is sometimes called 'contemplation'.

Stabilizing and analytical meditations are usually combined within a single meditation session. For example, as you prepare to meditate on your breathing rhythm, as in 'anapana' (a stabilizing meditation), it is helpful to spend a few minutes clarifying your state of mind and motivation for engaging in that session, which involves analytical thought. During both analytical and stabilizing meditations, your mind will frequently wander, constantly causing you to bring your attention back to your breath, as an anchor for your mind. At times it may be difficult to do this, at which point a return to a period of analyzing your state of mind will help.

During a session of analytical meditation, when you reach the point of intellectual understanding, it is then appropriate to let go of the thought process and focus your attention solely on associated feelings that arise. You will then arrive at a combined intellectual and experiential insight, causing your mind to become 'one' with the object of your meditation. This is unlikely to happen the first time you try it but, with repetition, sooner or later it will.

Your level of success will depend upon your depth of concentration, which will improve through regular practice. Regularity is actually more important than quantity, because your mind is strongly influenced by habitual patterns. If you do it regularly, your mind will come to expect it. This is how both good and bad habits are formed. So how long should a meditation session last? Start with five or ten minutes and build up to thirty minutes, ending your session before fatigue, aching knees and bottoms, and boredom set in. Do not push yourself too hard because as soon as it becomes a burden you won't do it. On some days you will experience more distractions and discomforts, while on other days you will be serene and focused. This is normal. View the troublesome sessions as opportunities to explore and grow. Also, you may often believe that you are making no progress, but think long-term. Results take time.

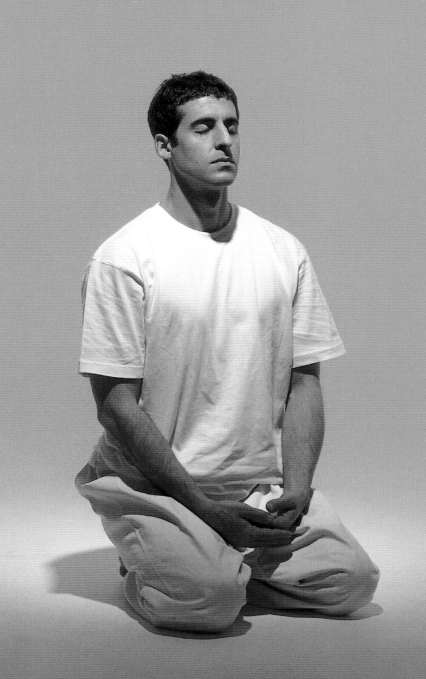

Impermanence

Nothing lasts forever, and all things are subject to change. Even a mountain will eventually erode away. This is impermanence, of which we all have an innate appreciation and understanding. Indeed, we have solid experience of it when we have lost something or are disappointed in some way. However, when things are going well, we tend to forget about the impermanent nature of things.

Our natural tendency is to strive for order, permanence and certainty. Thus, until we gain a proper understanding of impermanence, we will tend to feel that we are victims of the unpredictability of life. So, rather than expending our energies trying to control everything, an understanding of impermanence teaches us to be responsive to all things, but to hold on to nothing.

A greater appreciation of the reality of impermanence will naturally come about through the practice of mindfulness, and a truly deep and profound understanding of it is considered a major step towards a significant expansion of consciousness. Therefore, the contemplation of impermanence is a widely practiced analytical meditation, especially within the Buddhist traditions.

One may be tempted to think of stabilizing and analytical meditation as hierarchical levels of practice, with analytical contemplation ultimately offering a deeper potential for true understanding. Intellectual understanding is no more or less true than experiential understanding. Both are, in a way, two sides of the

of time, but which always subside or move. All sensations, whether pleasant, unpleasant or neutral, are given equal attention. In the beginning, only the more gross sensations such as pain and temperature might be perceived, but as mindfulness increases, we become more mindful of our relationship, attitudes and reactions to those sensations. As the practice develops, an enhanced appreciation of the nature of change and the inherent non-solidity within the body is gained. With experience, meditators can skip or minimize the scanning stage and simply allow their consciousness to be drawn to sensations wherever they arise.

This sounds simple, and it is, but as usual, it is not easy. Our mind, if not 'encouraged', much prefers to daydream and fantasize. For most people, especially if they live busy lives, it takes several days for them to build up to this type of meditation. Therefore, it is best done within a retreat environment of ten days or so.

Life is mostly unsatisfactory

What appears to motivate many people to embark upon meditation is the realization that life is basically unsatisfactory. Again, we know this at an intellectual level, because even if life is great now, we know that sooner or later we will die, and we really do not want to go through that. If for some reason we do want to die, then it must be because life is very unsatisfactory at present. So, because we want to be happy, we want to be free from the causes of discontent. By observing and contemplating discontent, we see that dissatisfaction is an integral component of our lives, and the amount of suffering in the world is incalculable. For example, just by considering the wildlife in your garden, it becomes clear that all creatures are basically trying to kill each other or trying to avoid being killed, with a little eating and reproducing going on in between. We might (or might

same coin. Both practices give 'insight' in different ways. For example, an immediate experiential insight into impermanence can be achieved through the stabilizing practice of drawing the mind to various sensations that arise within your body during meditation. An obvious sensation is the postural, knee and foot pain that may result from sitting still. The interesting thing is that these pains not only arise but also subside if they are observed rather than fought.

A method of insight (vipassana) meditation that has spread out of Burma from the Theravada Buddhist tradition emphasizes the mindfulness of bodily sensation as a core practice. The method involves a period of anapana initially to stabilize the mind, followed by the resting of one's mind upon any sensation that arises in the body. One technique to facilitate this process is to scan the body from head to feet in a specific sequence (a sort of 'active' stabilizing meditation), which tends to highlight sensations of varying intensities lasting varying lengths

not!) be in a less acutely blind or desperate situation, but still we find that almost everything we do is based on some underlying element of fear: fear of not being accepted, fear of being 'left on the shelf', fear of losing out, and so on. And what does fear imply? It implies that we suspect the cause of our own suffering is nearby, so we want to side-step out of its way.

We can be happy and contented for very long periods of time, but in a way, that can add to our problem. Being too comfortable makes us complacent. Why strive for anything, if it is all there at hand? That is fine if it will always be there, but we need to realize that the good times will not last forever. They may not even last into the next second, because the future is completely unpredictable.

We have three choices:

- We can become completely paranoid about our situation and life in general, worrying about suffering all the time, and feel guilty about any form of pleasure and happiness that might creep into our miserable existence.
- We can turn a blind eye to all sufferings and levels of discontent while things are going well, and deal with any pain when it 'unexpectedly' arises.
- We can do what it takes to truly understand the nature and inevitability of suffering, so that we can deal with it with equanimity.

On the surface, this whole concept seems a bit gloomy. "We're going to die"; "death is probably painful"; "life itself is full of anguish; if not now, sooner or later it will be". The point is, life does contain suffering. Pain and disappointment do not hurt less just because you did not see them coming. Worrying about their presence and inevitability also does not help. Quite the contrary. So what can we do? We can learn to understand and accept them, and meditating on the nature of suffering is a good way forward.

Meditation does not aim to reject or anaesthetize pain, or help us escape from life. Rather, it gives us a deeper understanding so that we can accept life with grace. Certain sufferings are inevitable for all of us: grief, illness, death, separation, rejection and so on. Other sufferings arise out of our narrow vision of life: our lack of wider understanding, which gives rise to fear, anger, envy and other emotional states. Mindfulness of suffering is not about dwelling upon discontent, but a means to help us understand that both avoiding and grasping create suffering for us. Meditation can therefore help us to learn about the nature of suffering and the means to reduce its impact on ourselves through the development of balance, understanding and compassion.

As an analytical contemplation on suffering, just remind yourself that everything is cyclic. Therefore, if you are suffering a painful low, it has to be balanced

by a euphoric high, and vice-versa. Part of the problem is the contrast between the high and the low. Meditation will encourage us to dwell more in the mid-point between those extremes, which, on balance, is much more 'satisfactory'.

The ultimate goal of meditation practice in eastern philosophical traditions is to get out of the cycle of suffering and euphoria altogether; to reach a state of 'liberation' from it all. Whether or not you achieve that ideal in this life, the practice of meditation clearly leads to a deeper sense of content. You need to do it regularly to experience what this means. Also, observe those who are really doing it whole-heartedly and extensively. They generally exhibit more sustained joy and contentment than the average person.

Selflessness

The more one meditates and the more one is more mindful in daily life, the greater the sense of 'connectedness' to all other things. The experience of self becomes inclusive of all things rather than exclusive. What is self anyway? Ponder that question; it is a good analytical contemplation.

A useful way of developing the sense of selflessness further is to consider whom you love and respect, and

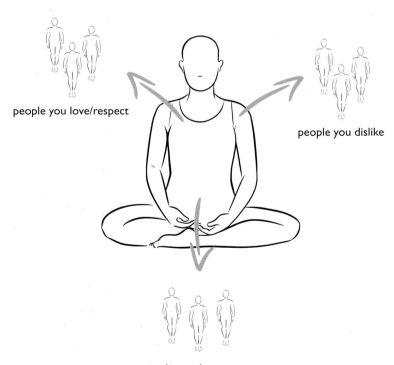

people you love/respect

people you dislike

people to whom you are indifferent

gradually widen the net. Probably you love yourself. If you think you do not, contemplate that notion and you should find that what you really mean is you dislike certain traits about yourself. At heart you want to change those traits. Why? Because you love yourself; if not, why would you bother wanting to change?

Next, consider who else you love and respect. Probably they will be your parents or children and other close friends. You dislike your parents? No! It just hurts to know that you do not get on with them, or they have favored someone else rather than you. If you did not love them, their indifference to you would not bother you so much.

When you look closely, you will see that you categorize people into three groups: those you love and/or respect (in varying degrees), those you dislike and/or do not respect (in varying degrees), and those to whom you are completely indifferent. In a way, people in the latter group are the ones who exacerbate your isolation, because at least you have some connection with and acknowledgement of the people in the other groups, whether in a positive or negative way.

Actually, another good contemplation exercise is to consider why you dislike certain people. Most people find that they dislike certain people mainly because they have the same irritating traits they see within themselves. In other words, they cannot bear to be reminded of themselves. Once again, the long-term solution is acceptance. Once accepted, things usually seem to improve. Try it and see.

So, widen your net to include those people you quite like. Add in those you dislike and reflect on the certainty that they are somebody's son or daughter. They could just as easily have been your son or daughter if time and space had worked out differently. Lastly, include all those to whom you are indifferent. That is more difficult, because you do not have such

a strong point of reference about them on which to latch your mind. This is a classic technique and it works well. It gets easier the more you do it. You could call it a love and compassion meditation.

Wisdom

Wisdom is really the insight gained through your life experience. It is not the knowledge, but the experiential understanding. In other words, you can be clever without being wise, and you can be wise without being an academic genius.

Meditation simply causes you to be more awake within life, so that more of your life is actually noticed by you. Therefore, it makes sense that meditation will lead to greater wisdom. Wisdom arises out of awakening. Total wisdom is the removal of all shadows, of all darkness. That is why it is called 'enlightenment'.

Enlightenment is a process characterized by a gradual expansion of consciousness, although this process is by no means smooth and regular. One can get to a level of awareness and then slip back and lose some of it. Diligent meditation practice is required to regain the momentum but, ultimately, consolidated progress will be made. However, the final step between not quite being fully enlightened and being fully enlightened may or may not be characterized by a sudden 'dawning.' We all occasionally experience these mental transitions on a small scale, hence the expression "it suddenly dawned on me." Imagine the whole answer to creation just 'dawning' on you! However, until the big 'dawning' comes, if and when it will, do not underestimate the value of the gradual expansion of wisdom to be gained by your daily meditation practice. It is well worth the effort.

AFFIRMATIONS

Affirmations can be used to persuade your subconscious to accept some personal quality to which you aspire, enabling that quality to become a reality. This is achieved by repeating some concise affirming words that embody your aspiration. For example, if you want to be clearer in speech because even mildly stressful situations cause you to stammer a little, you might repeat an affirmation such as: "My throat and chest are relaxed; my speech is clear and precise."

Such affirmations work better if they are repeated three times, three times per day at regular times. For example, you could say to yourself: "My throat and chest are relaxed ..." three times on waking, three times after lunch and then three times before you go to bed. In this way, the affirmation is repeated nine times per day. You can choose whether to say it aloud, say it in your head, or write it down. Occasionally writing your affirmations down, then burning them, with the clear intention that the affirmation is released into the 'ether' or the 'void', can work well.

Most of us believe that we need to give in order to receive. Therefore, in order to manifest the full fruit of your aspiration through affirmation, it is good to offer something back in return. Consequently, if you add

" ... I give that I shall receive" or "I give so that this is so" after each affirmation, it will remind you to do useful and generous things more often than you would otherwise have done. It is amazing what a difference this makes, and the spin-off is that you become a more generous and thoughtful person.

In the context of spiritual practice, affirmations are useful for reminding yourself of your spiritual aspirations, which are to manifest the highest virtues within yourself. For example, you might say to yourself "I shed my ignorance and emerge into the light" or "I speak only the truth". Remember to add "I give so that this is so".

The concept of affirmations is incredibly simple, yet amazingly effective. In many spiritual disciplines the reciting of mantras is practiced partly because they are making subtle affirmations to the subconscious (see mantras on pages 106–129). For example, in the Vedantic yoga tradition, the word 'Siva' (pronounced sheeva) is considered the allegorical embodiment of all the qualities necessary for the destruction of negative traits, to make way for their replacement with positive traits. To the Hindu, the same word is the name of Lord Siva, a deity who embodies the same qualities. So repetition of the Sanskrit mantra "OM Namah Sivaya"

invokes an affirmation for the destruction of negativity within oneself.

Affirmations can also therefore be a tool for reiterating your connection with deities or other aspirants whom you trust will support you in your spiritual quest. In that role they become a type of prayer. A good example of this is when Buddhists say "I take refuge in the Buddha, the Dharma and the Sangha." With these words they are affirming their connection with, and their aspiration to be like, the Buddha, to understand and live up to the Buddhist teachings (the Dharma), and to affirm their support for the work and aspirations of the custodians of those teachings (the Sangha).

Aspirations are also an effective way of reminding yourself why you are on your chosen spiritual path. For example, you might be drawn to the Mahayana Buddhist concept of donating the 'merits' of your practice as a catalyst for helping others to become enlightened, or at least to become as free from suffering as possible. On that path you would frequently say to yourself something like: "The purpose of my life is to free all living beings from all their problems and the causes of their problems ...," to which you could also add "...and to bring all beings peace and happiness."

Devotion in the context of spiritual practice tends to imply some form of belief and surrender to a higher immortal being, such as a god. That is, a being who inherently possesses all the attributes to which the devotee aspires, and more. This view suggests that devotion is synonymous with religion. However, devotion can also apply to non-theistic icons such as a Buddha, who has, within the same mortal limitations as you or I, attained 'realization' through spiritual practice. Thus, such an icon is selected to remind the devotee of his or her potential for reaching the same goal.

Devotion, therefore, usually has a 'being' as the object of devotion. But devotion can also be directed towards a more abstract focus, such as the 'ideal' of compassion or universal love. This sort of devotional practice could be called a 'humanistic' approach. However, most people find it easier to visualize an entity upon which their ideals can be projected.

Like all meditation methods, devotion requires and develops one-pointed concentration. Fundamentally, it uses the selected deity, icon or ideal as the focus, rather than something more neutral, such as a flame or the breath. How the focus is applied depends on one's preferences and mental characteristics. Some people like to use words that represent deities or ideals, hence we have devotional mantras. Others like to focus on images of deities, or patterns representing perfected spiritual qualities (mandalas). Physical gestures, such as prostration, can also be used.

Devotion is not truly meditative if it is blind devotion. Blind devotion is an abdication of personal responsibility, often based on fear or some other insecurity. Rather than expand awareness, blind devotion can dull your mind into the narrow vision of the zealot. In other words, devotion is better used as a tool rather than as a prop.

Devotion requires a degree of faith. This is not quite the same as belief, because it is not based on irrefutable opinions or certainties. Here, faith refers to

the optimism that will sustain us in our meditation practice. Whenever our actions have tangible results, for example, when we feel calmer and happier within our practice, then our faith in that practice is reinforced. Faith is therefore open to constant re-evaluation in the light of our own experiences.

Initial faith may coexist with doubt, as we evaluate our meditation in terms of 'success' or 'failure'. With time, we begin to recognize that the 'ups' and 'downs' of our meditation efforts are the natural order of things. Consequently, we learn not to be swayed by such oscillations. Eventually we gain an ability to accept whatever comes our way as an opportunity to learn and grow. Faith, therefore, really refers to an acquired confidence in what we are doing, based on the gathered experience of doing it. In that light, it can be seen as a quiet energy that sustains our spiritual momentum.

Visualization within meditation involves holding one-pointed attention on some form of selected imagery. This serves three purposes:

- To increase skills in one-pointed concentration. For example, holding the image of a candle flame in your 'mind's eye', then progressing to more complex images as your abilities improve.
- To facilitate specific movements or 'openings' of energy within the body, as commonly practiced in Daoist meditations (see pages 175–177), where pathways of 'life force' are influenced. Also, in *raja yoga*, to activate or 'open' one of the chakras, or energy centres (see page 96).
- To focus our attention on the qualities to which we aspire, as embodied in the visual image of a being or deity who possesses these qualities, or in a mandala that evokes these attributes.

Some people are able to visualize things easily whilst others find it difficult. It depends on whether or not you have a visual imagination. Either way, the ability to hold an image within your mind takes some practice. Developing any skill is best approached by starting from a point of simplicity and systematically progressing to the more complex. Therefore, taking a very straightforward image is a good way to start.

Candle gazing (Trataka)

One of the easiest images to visualize is a candle flame. Most people will find that gazing at a candle flame for a few seconds, followed by closing the eyes and maintaining the image is fairly easy. If the mental image fades, it is easy to open the eyes and look at the flame again to re-establish the link. Practice will soon give the ability to hold the image for longer.

Candle gazing or 'Trataka' is a yoga purification technique for cleansing the eyes. If you are performing it for that reason, you should gaze steadily at a candle flame placed at eye level a few feet away, ideally without blinking, until the eyes water. Some other mildly bright object, such as a coloured 15-watt light bulb, can be substituted if desired. The eyes should then be washed with cold water.

If Trataka is to be performed as a meditation rather than as a cleansing exercise, you should proceed as follows:

1 Place a candle or mildly bright object a few feet away at eye level, in a place free from draught (so that the flame is not disturbed).
2 Sit comfortably (see pages 35–39). Keep your posture relaxed, but erect, and gaze at the flame for a few seconds. Then close your eyes.
3 Keep the image of the flame firmly established in your 'mind's eye', maintaining as much detail about the flame's contour, brightness and general appearance as possible.
4 Repeat this procedure of gazing followed by visualizing as many times as feels comfortable. Whenever extraneous thoughts creep in, you can imagine those thoughts falling into the flame to be consumed in fire. As time goes on, you can shorten the time gazing at the flame and extend the time holding the image in your mind. Eventually you will be able to dispense with the physical flame altogether.

Sanskrit OM built up
in 3 stages

Tibetan OM built up in
4 stages

Building up complex images takes more practice. One method is to take the Sanskrit written character for OM, the universal sound. Stare at it in the same way as in the candle gazing exercise. The character is quite simple, so you may easily be able to recreate it in your mind. If not, build it up in stages. The Tibetan symbol for OM is slightly more difficult, so that represents a good progression. Once a clear and sustained image of either of these symbols is achieved, you could then follow this with contemplating the symbolism and meaning of OM (see pages 113–115 for more information about OM).

As your visualization skills develop, try doing a similar exercise with an image of your face, or if that distracts you, the face of somebody else, preferably someone for whom you have neutral feelings. You can use a photograph of the chosen face, or if the face belongs to you, you could sit in front of a mirror. This exercise can also be done with a partner, where you stare at each other's face before trying to build up a picture of it with your eyes closed. However, make sure you have the other person's cooperation and consent!

Using an icon from one's spiritual path will provide an excellent object of focus, because it will add the quality of connecting with that image at a devotional or energetic level. This type of practice is well developed in Tibetan Buddhism, particularly the tantric practices, which emphasize the rapid transformation of consciousness through visualization, symbols and ritual.

THE ROLE OF MEDITATION IN THE HEALING ARTS

When you talk to someone who has come to you for help, your ability to offer reassurance and give clear instructions are necessary tools of the trade. Likewise, for manual therapists, when you put your hands upon someone else's body, the actual mechanics of contact, such as the level of pressure and rhythm of movement, are essential ingredients for good bodywork. However, these are not the only factors that will have a bearing on how your counseling or touch is received. Your state of mind is also very important. Your attitude to the receiver, your reasons for practicing a healing art, your emotional disposition and your ability to remain focused are all critical elements.

When applying any form of healing technique, be it a word of advice or the application of pressure, you must be aware not to hurt the receiver. Conversely, you should not be so timid with your approach as to lack effectiveness. Somewhere between the two extremes is a line. The recognition of this line requires sensitivity, and sensitivity demands a focused mind.

If you are a bodyworker and you become distracted whilst handling the receiver's body, you will miss the signals that indicate whether or not you should continue to increase or decrease the pressure or the stretch. One way of keeping your mind focused is to go slowly and ask the receiver to tell you when you are entering the 'discomfort zone'. Due to the often extremely relaxing nature of many touch-based therapies, however, the receiver may put up with moderate pain and not bother to say anything until the pain is too much to bear. A healing touch does not need to be painful. If you are alert to the reactions of your touch, you will eventually learn to recognize the line between effectiveness and discomfort. The same applies to verbal counseling.

So how can you stay focused? If you are a bodywork therapist, you must work on your own body in some way to ensure you can remain comfortable throughout the session. If you are experiencing discomfort, you will be focusing on your own pains and unable to focus fully on the receiver's reactions to your touch. Also, whether you are a bodywork therapist or a counsellor, you would do well to adopt a method that trains your mind to remain more single-focused or one-pointed and less prone to wandering. There are many meditation, yoga, qigong (see pages 13–15, 95–96, 147–205 respectively) and mindfulness practices that you could adopt, some of which will be explored throughout this book.

PREPARING TO MEDITATE

Eastern countries, particularly Tibet and those of the Indian subcontinent, have a particularly strong tradition and cornucopia of meditation methods compared to that of western countries. Through the science and practice of yoga, the Indians developed a variety of sitting positions designed specifically to aid meditation and breathing exercises.

Sitting positions are generally preferred because they make it easier to remain still with an upright torso, thus enabling unrestricted breathing and alertness. Standing positions are useful for specific moving meditations, which are described later in this book. Lying down is useful in a few visualizations, but tends to induce sleepiness. For meditation, and any form of visual imagery, you need to be relaxed and alert at the same time. A relaxed but vertical spine within an upright posture is by far the most conducive position for this.

Most people will find sitting in a chair perfectly adequate, but for those who are able and happy to sit on the floor, the most common floor positions used by meditators are described and illustrated here. Choose the position you find most comfortable, because if you are not comfortable, you will be unable to focus your mind on anything other than your physical discomfort.

The three most well-known seated postures are the easy posture, the perfect posture and the lotus posture. These are described below in order of increasing difficulty.

The easy posture (Sukhasana)

This simply means sitting on the floor with your legs crossed. However, unless your knees are resting on the floor in this position, your pelvis will tend to tilt back slightly, causing fatigue in your lower back. For that reason, most people find it more comfortable to sit on a firm cushion to raise the buttocks a little.

In this position, as in all the positions described, keep your back erect and straight, though not rigidly so, with your head vertically in line with your back and your chin level. If your belly and chest feel like they want to collapse, try sitting on a thicker, firmer cushion.

The perfect posture (Siddhasana)

Sit on the floor. Bend your left leg and, grasping the ankle, draw the foot in against your perineum (between the anus and the scrotum or vulva). Now bend your right leg and place that foot in the crevice between the calf and the thigh of the left leg. Reverse the leg positions if you find that more comfortable. If both knees are not on the floor, either raise your buttocks onto a firmer, higher cushion, or revert to an easier posture.

Note: If your feet are not clear of your thighs when you sit in the lotus posture, you should only use the position for short periods of time to avoid straining the ligaments on the outer edges of your feet.

The lotus posture (Padmasana)

This is the most famous of the eastern postures used by yogis for meditation. Most westerners find it very difficult to get into and uncomfortable to maintain. It offers the most stability, but if it is painful and therefore distracts your mind, forget about it.

For those who want to sit in this position, sit on the floor with both legs extended. Bend one leg and grasp your ankle, pulling your foot against your perineum. Your knee should be flat on the floor. If it is not, you should abort the attempt immediately. Next, bend the other leg, grasp the ankle, and draw the foot up high on the thigh of the other leg as near as possible to your groin. Now try to lift the other foot

from the perineum onto the opposite thigh. Ideally, your feet should be well beyond the outer edge of your thighs, so that you can move your feet and ankles without restriction. This is possible for most Indians, because a racial characteristic for them is that their lower legs are proportionally longer in relation to their thighs than is the case for most westerners. Consequently, if you are a westerner seemingly able to do the lotus position, but the outer edges of your feet are not clear of your thighs, you will eventually weaken the ligaments on the outer edges of your feet. My advice therefore is to choose another position.

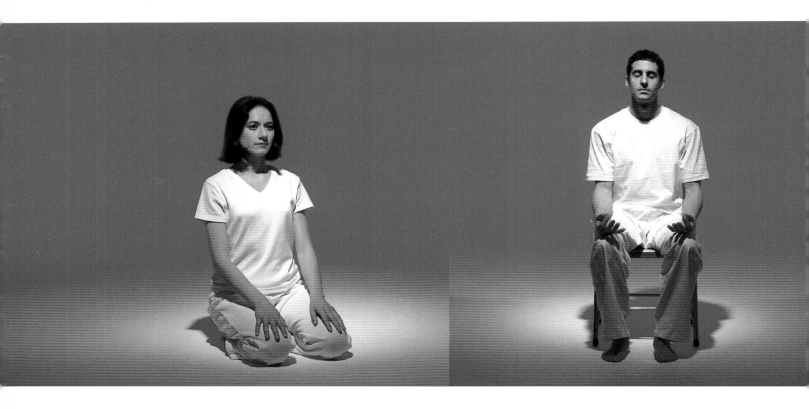

Kneeling (Vajrasana)

This posture is often used by many Zen meditators of the Japanese tradition, who call this position Seiza. It is also a yoga position known as the thunderbolt posture. It places the back, chest and head in an excellent position. The problem most people have with it is that it can create pain in the ankles if held for too long. Padding under the instep and/or sitting astride a bolster can solve this.

The position is very simple. Kneel so that you are sitting on your heels with your knees spread no more than the width of your fist (a little wider if you are sat astride a bolster). Your heels should be wider apart than your toes. The toes of each foot can be almost touching, touching or crossed slightly. Choose according to comfort.

Sitting in a chair (Egyptian posture)

Sitting on a bench or a straight-backed chair with the soles of your feet on the ground is known as the Egyptian posture. The seat of the chair should be about the same height as your lower legs, so that your thighs are parallel to the ground. A seat a little higher is better than a seat a little lower, because the latter will cause your lower back to sag backwards, causing pain and fatigue after a while. The important thing, as with all meditation postures, is to keep your body steady, with your back, head and neck in a relaxed but vertical alignment.

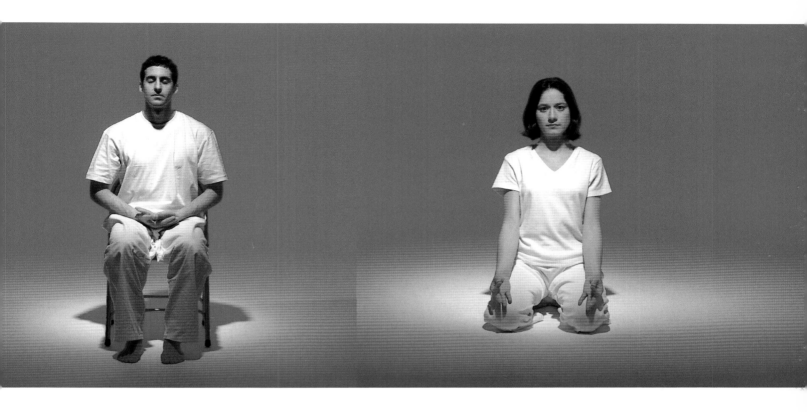

Hand positions for seated postures

Several hand positions are possible for use within any of these seated postures. One method is to place the back of your left hand in the palm of your right hand, with both hands resting in your lap. The thumbs either overlap, left over right, or touch at their tips to form a rough oval or triangle. In the perfect posture or lotus posture, the back of the right hand may rest on your upturned heel. If you are left handed, rest your right hand on top of your left hand. The idea is that your active hand is immobilized.

Another comfortable hand position is to have the backs of your hands simply resting on your thighs, near your knees, palms up. A more classical version of this is to have the forefinger and thumb of each hand touching to form rough circles, with the other fingers extended. Possibly you might find it more comfortable to have your palms facing down upon your thighs, or even on the arms of a comfortable straight-backed chair. Your comfort is by far the most important factor. The nuances of the specific hand position variants are significant for certain advanced meditation techniques, but not significant enough to worry about within the context of this book. Having said that, you may well find that during specific meditations, your hands automatically gravitate towards one or other of the variations mentioned.

Standing

Standing, so that your spine, head and neck can be held erect, in a relaxed way, without incurring fatigue, is essential for the various "meditations in movement" described later in this book. The basic standing position that acts as the starting point for these meditations requires that you stand with your feet about hip width apart, or slightly wider if you find that more comfortable. Your feet should be parallel rather than splayed apart, with knees slightly bent or 'unlocked.' Imagine that your pelvis is a bowl of water resting on the top of your legs (which it is, in a way). Keep your 'pelvic bowl' level so that the water you imagine within it neither spills from the front nor from the back. Then ensure you have equal weight distributed between the balls of your feet and your heels. Some people feel more balanced by feeling fractionally more weight, say two per cent more, falling through the balls of their feet. Experiment and choose for yourself.

Now, feel that your spine is growing out of your pelvis like the stem of a water reed growing up through water, allowing the spaces between each vertebra to 'float' open and apart. Your arms will naturally float slightly away from your body, just enough so that air or 'water' can circulate around your armpits. This image will engender a tremendous feeling of lightness and straightness within your spine, as you feel the buoyancy of water negating the effect of gravity on your posture.

Keep the posture thus attained, and then imagine a cord attached to the top of your head, just to the rear of the head's midpoint. Feel that a mild traction is applied to that cord which further "opens and lengthens" your neck. You will need to surrender your neck to the lengthening image by consciously relaxing it. Parting your teeth and relaxing your tongue helps this considerably. Then imagine that the flesh of your

body hangs down like heavy leaves around an ever-lengthening central stem, which is your spine, while simultaneously feeling that your legs and feet are full of sand, so that your feet appear to sink a little into the ground.

To complete the image, keep feeling that your legs are full and grounded, but your torso is a hollow cavity, light and buoyant between the heavier 'leaves' of skin and the even more buoyant spinal column. Going through the process to get to this point is a meditation in itself. Do not worry if you forget a few details. It will all come together spontaneously, the more you practice the bits you can remember.

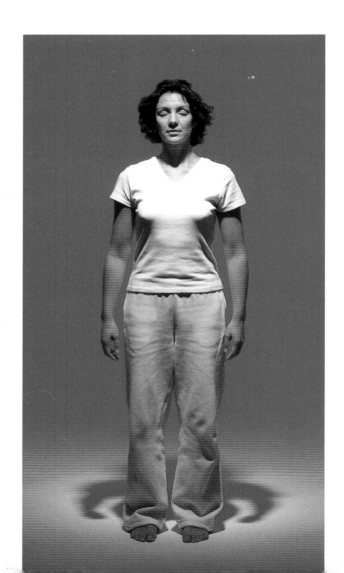

Lying down (savasana – the 'corpse' posture)

Lying down is used more as a method to move from total stress to a state of reasonable equanimity, through deep relaxation techniques, rather than as a position for practicing specific visualizations. Meditation requires a certain level of alertness that is not easy to maintain when lying down. Almost everyone is used to sleeping when lying down, so sleep is what tends to come when adopting that position. Therefore, going through the process of letting go through a series of relaxation exercises whilst lying down is used when you are too tired to go through the same procedure sitting up. It can also be a comfortable position to adopt if someone else is talking you through a visualization, or if listening to a recorded visualization.

To perform savasana correctly, lie flat on your back with your arms palms up, slightly away from your body. Your heels should be just touching, if comfortable, with your toes apart. However, if you find it more comfortable, having your heels up to 10cm/4in apart is permissible. Your lower jaw should be totally relaxed, never clenched, and your tongue totally passive. Your eyes must be closed, and it helps to cover the eyes with a dark cloth. Better still is to use a cloth slightly weighted with small beanbags because slight, even pressure on the eyeballs activates a relaxation reflex via the vagus nerve (a cranial nerve), which causes the body and mind to relax. One mental command that many people find useful is to say, "my eyes sink deeply into my eye sockets, resting against my brain."

Once in this position, doing anapana mindfulness breathing (see pages 9–10) is useful, or consciously breathing quite deeply but finely, trying to create as little disturbance around your nostrils as possible (that is, preventing nostril flaring and sensations of heat). If Savasana is done successfully, you will get a definite feeling that energy is flowing from the back of the head towards the heels, not the other way round. Ten minutes of this will be highly rejuvenating for mind and body, with the bonus of having centered your mind ready for meditation in seated or standing positions.

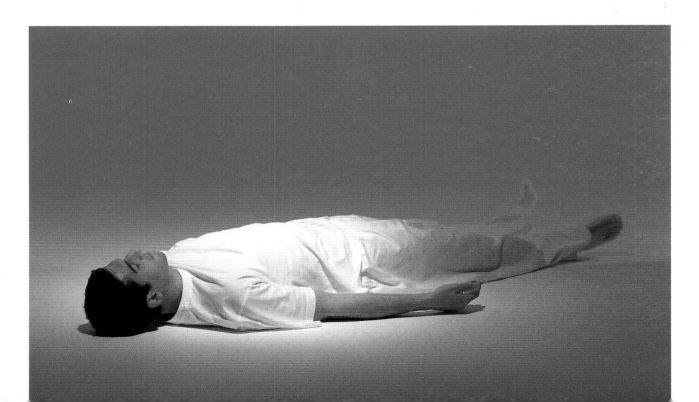

It is extremely important to do everything you can to encourage within yourself a greater equanimity of mind and one-pointed mental focus. It makes sense, therefore, to minimize potential stress-inducing situations, especially immediately prior to entering a meditation exercise or giving any form of healing to others. So if you have to travel to get to your place of meditation, allow plenty of time and remember to practice mindfulness of breath on the way. That should help.

You cannot always choose where to meditate, but if you are in a position to select the optimum location and can influence the ambience of the room, then here are a few suggestions.

If you have the space, a separate room used solely for meditation is ideal. The reason for keeping this space separate from other activities is because the feeling within a defined space, especially an enclosed space, will gradually become influenced by the activities that take place there. If a room is used predominantly for bitter arguments, then an argumentative atmosphere will permeate the feel of that room. On the other hand, if the room is used solely for meditation, then the room will take on the same peaceful feeling associated with meditation.

Creating an ambience of peace and serenity in a meditation room has many clear advantages. Firstly, when the positive ambience of the room builds to a sufficient level, the room will become like a sanctuary for you. You will find that, upon entering the room, the familiar feeling of serenity associated with that particular space will override any negative feelings you may have at that time. For example, if you have been working downstairs on a stressful project, or you have had a disagreement with your partner, entering your sanctuary will make you feel as if all that is far away. You will, in effect, have entered a 'bubble' that seems divorced from the normal stresses of life.

You may have experienced a similar effect when returning to a far-away holiday location. Sometimes, when you return to somewhere associated with vivid memories, those vivid memories come flooding back, pushing more routine memories and thought processes into the background of your mind. It feels like no significant time has elapsed since you were there before. You seem to have entered a 'bubble' which, in a way, lies outside of time and space. Your meditation room will also act as a 'bubble', and trigger feelings of tranquillity as soon as you enter it.

If you cannot reserve a whole room for meditation, try to reserve a space within a quiet room that is normally used for something not too frenetic or depressing. A good ambience will still begin to manifest itself there, but maybe not so quickly or strongly, because the space is not exclusively devoted to meditation. If you cannot reserve a corner solely for this purpose, at least try to meditate in the same place each time. Just going to that familiar location will trigger your mind to switch into mindfulness mode.

The contents of your meditation room

Once you have established a location for your meditation, what should you put in it? 'Not much' is my advice. Material clutter will clutter your mind. Clutter has its own ambience and, because, by definition, there is a lot of it, that ambience tends to be a conflicting mish-mash. Keep it clean and simple.

Sitting in a cold room is not much fun, so do keep the room warm. In addition, provide a blanket to keep yourself comfortable in case you begin to feel cold. Judicious placement of plants will enhance your room. Maybe have a few simple pictures on the wall, but nothing too evocative.

You might interpret these suggestions as a restriction on the expression of your personality. You may want to include art and décor that reflect the inner 'you'. But reflecting 'you' is not the point in this particular room. You have the rest of your home for that. Your meditation space must be as neutral as possible, free from metaphors about your personality. Remember, you want your 'bubble' to be independent from the rest of your life's ups and downs. However, if you are practicing meditation within a particular philosophical or religious system, certain icons of that system may be included in your room as dictated or guided by the rules or suggestions of that practice.

Keep your meditation space clean, simple and welcoming. Beyond that, you could consider the feng shui (energetic configuration) of the room, which is beyond the scope of this book, but there are many books on feng shui available if you would like to explore this further.

Choosing a location

Some people ask if it would be better to meditate in a really isolated position, such as a cave in the hills or mountains. If all your needs can be met, such as food, warmth, and someone to take care of your commitments and responsibilities elsewhere, then by all means go to the hills. However, it is more likely that you are not in that situation. Besides, this book is about using meditation to enhance your equanimity within the life you lead. It is not a manual for the ascetic monk or nun. Other books deal with that level of commitment.

To live our lives, we need to gain control of our minds so that we can experience all-pervading unity in our current situation. Mindfulness should therefore be practiced even in the midst of your most intense activity. If your senses are under control, inner peace can be achieved even in the noisiest, most crowded city.

ॐ

OVERCOMING OBSTACLES
TO MEDITATION

The biggest obstacles to your meditation practice will be lack of motivation, boredom, sleepiness, restlessness or excitement, discomfort and pain, negative thoughts, and lack of input from someone more experienced than you. As such, it is recommended that you seek out a good meditation teacher if and when the time comes for your meditation practice to progress. The qualities you should look for in a teacher include compassion, knowledge, humility, sincerity, insight, morality and the ability to explain clearly. Your meditation teacher should be someone who thoroughly understands how the mind works, based on his or her own practice. Do not be in any hurry to find your teacher. That person will show up when the time is right. Meanwhile, practice what I have suggested in this chapter, and allow your intuition to guide you a little.

The following pages highlight the common obstacles to meditation and offer solutions, including visualizations, as antidotes to those obstacles.

Sleepiness

Problem	Solution
Spine not straight	Hold spine straight, but not tense.
Head held too far forward	Hold head only slightly forward with chin tucked in.
Your mind habitually believing that closing your eyes means it is time to sleep	Open your eyes half-way and meditate with your gaze fixed on the floor some way in front of you.
Unexpected feeling of depression	Remember that thoughts and feelings come in waves so wait for them to pass rather than cling to them.
Room too dark	Increase the light slightly.

Sleepiness antidote visualization

If the above adjustments fail to stop you wanting to doze off, and you have a visual imagination, try this simple exercise before continuing with your session.

1 Imagine the bottom half of a large, hollow, white seed, about the size of half a tennis ball, in your lower belly 5cm/2in below your navel. Then picture the top half of a hollow, red seed, of similar size, deep in your solar plexus. Imagine your mind filling the space between the two seed halves.

2 Now visualize the two seed halves shrinking as they converge just in front of your spine at the level of your umbilicus. As they do so, your mind becomes fully encapsulated within this tiny red and white seed.

3 Visualize a hollow tube about one finger's width in diameter situated just in front of your spinal column, running from the base of your spine to the top of your head. Now imagine the seed shoots up through that tube to emerge above the crown of your head. The seed evaporates, allowing your mind to expand into, and merge with, a vast empty void. Dwell upon this experience for a few moments before returning to your original meditation.

Restlessness and excitement

Problem	Solution
Spine not straight	Hold spine straight, but not tense.
Head and chin held too high	Hold head only slightly forward with chin tucked in.
Being involved in a particularly exciting set of happenings at this time	Reflect upon the fact that excitement is always short-term. Feelings such as excitement come in waves, so wait for them to pass rather than cling to them.
Breathing too quickly and too shallow	Focus on your lower belly and observe your breathing as if it does not belong to you, and notice how it just happens without you having to exert any control over it.
Room too light	Decrease the light slightly.

Excitement antidote visualization

1 Do the first part of the red and white 'seeds at the navel' visualization in the same way as described for sleepiness (see page 50), up to the point where the seed halves shrink and converge with your mind inside it.

2 Dwell for a few moments on the feeling of 'being centered' and 'being grounded' created by the fact that your mind is now snuggled up inside a seed which itself is anchored deep in your belly. Then return to your original meditation.

Discomfort and pain

Problem	Solution
Incorrect posture	Experiment with your position. If you have lower back pain, sit on a higher and/or firmer cushion. Lean up against something firm if necessary.
Stress on knee or ankle through a cross-legged posture that is too extreme	Put cushions under your knees or kneel, or sit on a chair.
Tension from unresolved problems, worry or anger	Use the problem or emotion itself as the focus for your meditation. Also, imagine the pain evaporating from your body with each exhalation.

Pain antidote visualization

The 'body sweep' method can be very effective against pain. Imagine your consciousness as a gentle shower of cool water washing you down from head to feet, being fully aware of every part of your body as the 'shower' washes over it. Whenever your mind 'washes' into a painful area, imagine the pain is swept away. The hotter your pain, the cooler you should make your 'shower'.

If the pain does not go away, or does not become acceptable, just observe the pain and try to see it as just another sensation. Alternatively, mentally increase the pain as much as possible before returning to the original pain, which should then seem less intense.

If you cannot eliminate or accept the pain, stop the meditation and try again another time. If the pain persists between meditations, seek advice from a suitably qualified medical practitioner.

Negativity

Problem	Solution
No problem here. This simply means your mind is digging up thoughts, feelings and attitudes that are already present.	Bring your attention back to your breath, then use the negative thought as the object of your meditation.

Negativity can be 'hot,' producing feelings such as anger, resentment or jealousy, or it can be 'cold,' such as feeling sorry for yourself within depression, or being fixed in a state of melancholic grief.

Negativity antidote visualization

1 Imagine you are sitting neck-deep in a tub of warm water. As a negative thought arises, feel it soak out of your body (or out of the red and white seed behind your navel – see the sleepiness antidote visualization on page 50) into the surrounding water.
2 When the water becomes discoloured by your negative thoughts, imagine it emptying away, so that all those bad thoughts disappear down the drain. The dirtier the water, the better, because it means you are dredging out and expelling more and more negative thoughts.
3 Fill up the tub again, via an imaginary shower pouring onto your head. Repeat the exercise until no more negative thoughts arise and the water in the tub remains clean.

During subsequent meditations, when negative thoughts arise, do the same visualization and feel that you are washing out deeper and more subtle layers of mental dross.

Note: Avoid trying to repress feelings of negativity because they will only emerge again later, in an exaggerated form.

Negativity transformation exercises

Negativity may be something you want to expel, yet it is still your negativity. Therefore, your other option is to accept and transform it.

Allow the negative thought to enter your mind freely. More often than not, immediately you give such space to a negative thought it instantly loses its momentum, even before you need to go as far as observing any reactions you might have to it. This is especially true of 'hot' negativity such as anger or jealousy. The 'hot' negative thought is only likely to persist beyond the time of recognizing it if the situation that caused it is still underway, or recent enough to be overwhelming you emotionally. In other words, the cause and/or repercussions of your negative feelings are still in the present.

You probably would not be reading this book right now if you were in a 'hot' negative state of mind. So, as an experiment, imagine yourself angry, sad, resentful or envious. It is very difficult to get that gut-wrenching sensation, like you do when you really feel that way. However, next time you are genuinely feeling negative about something, affirm that fact to yourself. For example, if you are feeling angry, say to yourself "I am feeling angry." Then mindfully observe how that affects your body, especially your breathing and posture. It is very likely that, as a result of that simple recognition, the negative thought and its associated emotion will be neutralized.

Something like deep grief is more intractable. The way to address that is to do what has just been suggested under problem and solution. To transform it, you will need to deeply contemplate things like impermanence, the nature of time or the nature of grasping. However, do not grasp for a solution. On the contrary, let go (without trying to let go). This takes practice.

Strange bodily sensations

If you experience weird sensations such as your body shrinking or expanding, or your mind leaving your body behind, these are normal reactions of the mind to meditation, especially in the beginning stages. Therefore, you should experience them, then ignore them. They will fade away in due course. These sensations can become quite a thrill, but do not get attached to them or wish for them, otherwise they may become major distractions from your focus.

Meditation checklist

Get comfortable in your chosen posture.

Check and acknowledge your motivation and goal. (It might be simply to calm down.)

Before you leave your meditation, recall your goal to see whether or not you achieved it. For example, have you calmed down?

Allow much of what you have gained from your meditation to spill over into your daily life.

Dedicate your efforts and offer your gains to the welfare of others. This will really help to link your motivation for meditating with a sense of compassion, which in turn will help predispose your mind to meditation.

Meditation and healing

If you are a therapist or healer, and wonder if you should meditate at the same time as giving treatment, the best way to apply your mind while giving any form of healing, be it on a professional level, or simply giving some massage to a friend, is to be as mindful as possible of everything you experience and do throughout the session. Remember to bring your attention back to your breath when your mind wanders, and feel the slight movement of your lower belly as you breathe.

BREATHING AND CENTERING

It is not always easy to start meditating whenever you feel like it. You need to get your mind into the correct gear. Even observing the breath with the anapana method (see pages 9–10) may need to be preceded by some form of centering exercise if your mind is particularly scattered or apathetic. Basically you need to relax if you are buzzing, or wake up a bit if you are sleepy. If you are buzzing, you need to relax your body and mind. A very effective way to achieve this quickly is known as the 'tense-release' method.

PRELIMINARY CENTERING EXERCISES

Tense-release method

1 Adopt your preferred meditation posture, although if you have the space, lying down is easiest (see savasana on page 4).

2 Tense your whole body by simultaneously clenching your fists, face, back, buttocks and thighs, and curling your toes as you inhale. Then let go completely as you exhale.

3 As you inhale, stretch your face muscles by opening your mouth and eyes as wide as possible, and stretch open your palms, fingers and toes as much as you can. Exhale and relax.

4 Repeat this tensing and stretching sequence once or twice more.

5 Tense and relax individual areas of the body, beginning with your face: screw up your face muscles, then relax them. Tense and relax the rest of your body in the following order: face; shoulders; arms and hands; upper back; buttocks; thighs; calves; toes.

Salutations to the moon

Another good centering method is the standing exercise known as 'Salutations to the moon'. This is basically a sort of Indian qigong (energy work using movement, breathing techniques and meditation), utilized by some Indian yogis. It is particular good for people who want to involve their hands to help heal others, because it strongly focuses your mind upon your hands. As such, it is a useful, quick centering exercise to do immediately prior to giving any form of bodywork session. It also opens the lungs and mildly stretches the diaphragm, and serves as a basic but effective breathing exercise.

Do this exercise slowly, making sure that the breathing rhythm is not controlled, but allowed to subside into a relaxed and natural pace. The movements should follow the rhythm of the breath. That way, as you become more relaxed, the breathing will deepen and the movements will slow down. The breath should never chase after the movement, because that will make the breathing shallower and quicker and cause the movements to speed up.

Salutations to the moon exercise

1 Stand with your feet about hip-width apart, with knees unlocked and hands loosely by your sides.
2 Inhale as you raise your hands sideways to shoulder height.

3 Exhale as you place your palms together in front of your chest.
4 Inhale as you stretch your arms and fingertips out in front of you, arms straight.

5 Exhale as you stretch your arms overhead, arms straight, palms facing forward.

6 Inhale as you lower your arms sideways to shoulder height.

7 Exhale as you lower your arms by your side.

In addition to the centering exercises just described, there are many useful techniques based on controlling the breath, known as pranayama, from the tradition of Indian yoga. These exercises naturally center the mind, and some of them are described on the following pages.

'Prana' is the Sanskrit term used by Indian yogis to denote the power behind and within our breath. More broadly it is the vital force in every living being as well as the all-pervasive universal energy within every atom and every thought. It is therefore equivalent to the Chinese term qi and its Japanese equivalent ki.

Pranayama is the yoga science of breath control, which ultimately enables the yogi to tap the infinite well of universal energy. The sources of the word pranayama are prana (the life breath, life force or universal energy) and ayama (pause). Pranayama is the method of controlling the mind by controlled and measured breathing. For example, it is well known that there is a reciprocal relationship between our breathing and our emotions. When we are excited, our rate of breathing increases. When we are composed and centered, our breathing becomes slow, deep, calm and rhythmical. When we are living totally in the moment, such as when listening for the sound of a pin dropping onto the ground, our breathing is totally suspended (try this yourself). As such, it follows that if we can control our breathing pattern, we can strongly influence our state of mind. Pranayama exercises range from the very simple to the highly specialized methods used by experienced

yoga adepts. For our purposes, the safe and simple methods are sufficient.

Pranayama requires an erect but relaxed upright posture so that the lungs can expand freely, and the movement of the diaphragm is unrestricted. The same seated postures as used for meditation practice are used, so before you begin practising, select your preferred sitting position as outlined in chapter 2 (see pages 35–39).

Before commencing pranayama, your body should be clean. Sponge yourself down and rinse your mouth with water, clean your teeth and clear your nostrils by blowing each separately. Avoid heavy meals immediately before practicing, and loosen any constrictive clothing. Choose a quiet, ventilated area such as outside (weather permitting), in front of an open window, or at least in an airy room. Make sure you are warm enough because feeling cold will cause you to contract your chest muscles, and restrict your ability to breathe fully. Developing fuller breathing is one of the main reasons for doing pranayama.

Now that you have prepared yourself correctly, try the following exercises and note their specific effects.

The cleansing breath (Kapalabhati)

Kapalabhati is not actually considered to be a pranayama; it is really a purification practice designed to clear the sinuses and rid the nadis (the Sanskrit term for energy channels or meridians) of impurities. It enriches the bloodstream and improves circulation, strengthens digestion and is said to rejuvenate and prolong life. For this reason, it is a good exercise to perform before proceeding with other pranayama exercises. It also has the effect of cooling inflamed eyes. However, it is advisable to avoid this exercise if you have high blood pressure.

During this exercise, both inhalation and exhalation take place through the nose. Exhalation is accomplished by means of a quick and vigorous contraction of the abdominal muscles and diaphragm.

1 Take a few deep inhalations and exhalations through the nose.

2 Take a moderate breath through both nostrils, then retract your abdominal muscles and diaphragm with a sharp in-stroke that forces the air out of your nose rather like a sneeze . Immediately the exhalation is over, inhale again.

Exhalation should take about half the time it takes to inhale. Initially do it ten times at the rate of ten exhalations over five seconds. Rest for between 30 and 60 seconds breathing first deeply, then normally. Repeat two or three more times. As you get used to it with practice, increase the number of breaths in a round until you can do 20 or 30 inhalations and exhalations. You can increase the speed slightly as long as you maintain control of the balance between inhaling and exhaling. If you need to gasp for air, either during the exercise or between rounds, slow down. Your belly may feel slightly sore in the beginning, but this will soon pass as your abdominal muscles strengthen.

As you get used to kapalabhati breathing, you can refine your technique by trying to make it as silent as possible. The tendency in the beginning is to contract your nostrils as you exhale, causing you to sound like an old railroad steam engine. The trick is to relax your nostrils as you exhale, so that they are more open, allowing more air out. A classic image is to imagine you have a small feather or piece of fluff on the tip of your nose, and that with each exhalation the feather is only slightly dislodged rather than blasted away.

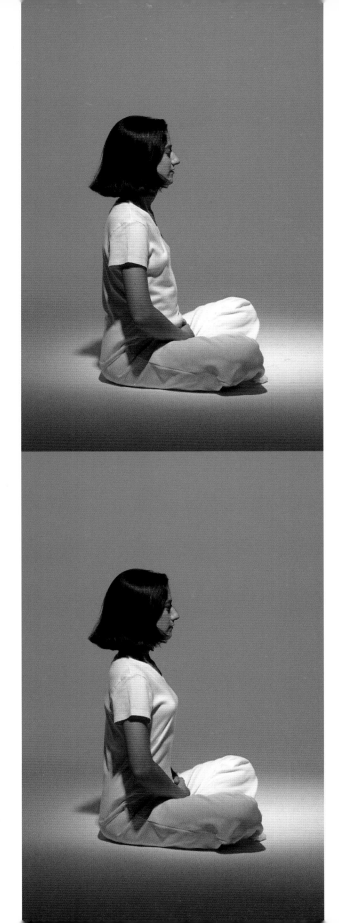

Simple alternate nostril breathing (Sukh Purvak, also known as Nadi Sodhana)

Like Kapalabhati, this exercise also aids digestion, enriches the blood and cleanses the nasal passages. It also tones and purifies the nadis (energy channels) and increases the appetite. However, its main relevance to the meditation and visualization practices outlined in this book is that it calms and concentrates the mind very quickly. It does this through breath entering the right nostril, which enters a nadi called the 'pingala nadi' (see illustration on page 137). This awakens us and heats the body, generally activating both body and mind. Breath entering the left nostril enters a nadi known as the 'ida nadi,' which pacifies and cools us.

Ancient yoga texts describe the ida and pingala nadis as criss-crossing through a central nadi in the vicinity of the spinal cord, known as the 'susumna nadi.' At intervals, the ida and pingala nadis cross through the susumna nadi at the level of energy vortices known as 'chakras' or energy centers. Interestingly, when seen in the context of modern physiological science, the ida and pingala nadis are located in the vicinity of the autonomic nervous system, which has two distinct aspects: the sympathetic branch, which activates us ready for action, and the parasympathetic branch, which sedates us ready for rest. We can therefore say that breath taken through the right nostril stimulates the sympathetic nervous system, which activates us, whereas breath taken through the left nostril stimulates the parasympathetic nervous system, which relaxes us.

Depending on our emotional state, our natural energy cycle and state of health, we will be taking slightly more air through one nostril compared to the other at any given time. The emphasis naturally shifts between nostrils about every two hours. However, when we are engaged in hyperactivity of some sort (sympathetic nerve mode), the breath slightly predominates through the right nostril (pingala nadi). When we are asleep (extreme sympathetic nerve mode), the breath slightly predominates through the left nostril (ida nadi).

Alternate nostril breathing equalizes the breath between the ida and pingala nadis, thus balancing the autonomic nervous system. As a result, we become alert but relaxed and centred, rather than lethargic or hyperactive and scattered. Consequently, it becomes much easier to achieve one-pointed focus of the mind.

Advanced yogis will be aiming to balance the prana (qi) within the ida and pingala nadis, using various methods and extensive practice, to the degree where it can enter the susumna nadi and activate a latent energy stored at the base of the spine called 'kundalini shakti,' which will then rise through all seven chakras, leading to enlightenment (see pages 138–139 for a full explanation). Our more modest aim at this stage is to use alternate nostril breathing to help focus our concentration. A clear description of this technique is given in an original yoga text entitled *Hatha Yoga Pradipika*, which has been translated as follows:

1 Sitting in the Padmasana posture (or a suitable alternative seated posture – see pages 35–39), the yogi should take air through the left nostril (closing the right one) and, keeping it confined according to one's ability (suspend the breath for a few seconds), it should then be expelled slowly through the right nostril.
2 Then, drawing air through the right nostril slowly, the belly should be filled, and after performing kumbhaka (suspension of the breath) as before, it should be expelled slowly through the left nostril.
3 Inhaling through the nostril through which it was expelled, and having restrained it (for a few moments), it should be exhaled through the other, slowly and not forcibly.

Sukh Purvak

(Simple Alternate Nostril Breathing, also know as Nadi Sodhana)

The *Hatha Yoga Pradipika* then goes on to say: "By practicing in this way, through the right and left nostrils alternately, the whole of the collection of nadis of the yamis (those who practice) become clean, i.e. free from impurities, after three months."

Do not force any phase of your breathing cycle during this exercise (or during any of the breathing exercises described here), especially with regard to the retention of breath phase. The ratio favoured by experienced yogis between inhalation, retention and exhalation is 1:4:2. In other words, you inhale for five seconds, hold the breath for twenty seconds and exhale for ten seconds. This is rather severe for most people, so you may prefer a more comfortable ratio of 1:1:1 or 1:1:2. To calm the mind, about five or six rounds should be sufficient, but do not hold the breath at all if you have high blood pressure.

The traditional method for closing the nostrils is to press the index and middle fingers against the palm and use the thumb to close one nostril and the ring finger and little finger to close the other nostril.

Sitkari and Sitali

These two breathing exercises specifically cool the body down as well as calm the nervous system. They also appease hunger and thirst. Therefore they are useful exercises to employ if uncomfortably hot conditions are making meditation difficult. The techniques basically consist of sucking in air over your tongue, which will cool your blood, because the tongue has a very rich supply of blood.

For people who can curl their tongue, sitali is more effective. For those who cannot, sitkari is better. Either technique can be repeated for six or seven rounds in succession. If you are particularly hot, repeat a series of rounds at intervals during your meditation session.

Sitkari technique

1 Place your tongue between your upper and lower rows of teeth, leaving a little space between your upper lip and tongue for air to be drawn in. This will produce a hissing sound.
2 Hold your breath for a second or two, then exhale through your nostrils.

Sitali technique

1 Curl your tongue into a trough and protrude it between your lips, sucking air in through that trough.
2 Draw your tongue back into your mouth so that you can breathe out through your nose.

What is consciousness? Who or what is meditating? From where does consciousness arise? These questions have preoccupied deep thinkers and analytical meditators for millennia. The following contemplations should prove to be useful tools to gain some basic insight into these questions, although they are unlikely to give you the full answers.

Within every philosophy or tradition that explores the mind, water is the most commonly used metaphor associated with consciousness. A few examples that come to mind are:

- Enlightened consciousness is an *ocean* of bliss.
- Thoughts are like the ripples on the surface of a *lake* that must be stilled to reveal your true reflection.
- If the surface of the *pool* is disturbed in any way, the bottom of the pool cannot be seen. Likewise, if the mind is agitated, we cannot *fathom the depths* of our mind.
- Liberation is about connecting with the *sea* of consciousness.

The following statements may act as catalysts for analytical contemplations about the nature of consciousness, through the metaphor of water.

WATER CONTEMPLATIONS

The flow of a river proceeds as an unbroken continuum, yet exhibits and initiates many changes and characteristics within itself and its surroundings throughout its course. Similarly, human beings continue from generation to generation, contributing an unbroken chain of genes to successive generations, evolving through the merging of genes – just as a river evolves and gains power as it merges with other rivers.

An active mind and body that allow for change and development are like a moving river that does not stagnate.

Oceans, which are literally deep, represent the hidden depths within our psyche. The depth of the ocean is hidden like the source of our consciousness, which originates somewhere at the dawn of time.

For us, water actually has five broad associations and influences, namely:

- water is the source of life
- water flows within us
- water purifies our tissues
- water governs our deep structures and resources
- water gives us power

Any of these five phrases about water can be used as a focus for analytical contemplation. In addition, the following meditations and affirmations mobilize and strengthen some of these qualities of water within us. Consequently, if through our meditations and contemplations we can 'connect' with water, we have a good chance of triggering a profound insight into consciousness.

Water is the source of life

This refers to the fact that all life on this planet ultimately originated in water. Life always has water within its structure, and life depends on water to survive. Water is therefore a universal bond shared by all living things. It is the thing that every plant and animal has in common.

We, like all living things, are literally from, of, and dependent on, water, which means that, through the energy of water, we are intimately connected with all life and with our environment. Water gives us the balance between hot and cold, dry and moist, rest and activity. If we fail to connect with this fact, we cut ourselves off from the source of our life and it will be difficult for us to find the energy to do what we want to do.

Source of life meditation

To increase our energy, we need to realize that we can connect with the limitless energy that is active all around us. As already discussed, this connection is ultimately dependent on water. The following meditation will help to forge this connection.

1 Stand with your feet slightly apart with your knees unlocked and your spine erect but relaxed. Your arms should be loosely relaxed by your sides, with a sense of space under your armpits. Alternatively, sit in any of the seated positions described earlier (see pages 35–39).

2 Imagine you are standing (or sitting) in a crystal-clear lake, with water up to your shoulders. Your feet (or buttocks) sink heavily into the floor of the lake.

3 Practice simple anapana breath awareness (see pages 9–10), focusing on your lower belly, below your navel, for a minute or two.

4 As you inhale very slowly, imagine you are drawing clear water into your lower belly, and imagine your arms floating slightly further outwards away from your body. Slowly exhale and allow your arms to sink back to your sides, feeling that the water you took in is released through your fingers and toes.

5 Form a clear picture of your kidneys in your mind's eye (see page 88). Then, as you inhale, allow your arms to float outwards from your body to the surface of the lake. You can actually allow your arms to move outwards if you like. As you do so, visualize water entering through your lower belly and filling your expanding kidneys. Then exhale, allowing your arms to sink down, releasing most of the acquired water through your fingers and toes, but retaining a little in your kidneys. Repeat this process three or four times, reflecting on the concept that water is the deep source of your life and of your vitality.

6 With your next inhalation and exhalation, clearly visualize your liver (see page 90). As you inhale, raising your arms, imagine some water from your kidneys being drawn into your liver. As you exhale, lower your arms and reflect on the concept that water is the deep source of your life and generates the vitality of your liver.

7 With your next round of breathing, visualize your heart. As you inhale, imagine some water from your kidneys being drawn into your heart. As you exhale, lower your arms and reflect on the concept that water is the deep source of your life and generates the vitality of your heart.

8 With your next full round of breathing, create the image of water moving from your kidneys into your lungs (see page 87).

9 If you have time, repeat this visualization cycle once or twice more. To finish, hold your hands over your lower belly and feel deeply connected to the water in the lake, to all life in the lake, and to all life everywhere.

Power meditation

To strengthen your will power and determination, that is, to strengthen the attribute of ocean-like power within you, try the following meditation.

1 Sit comfortably in your preferred meditation posture, drawing your awareness to your belly. Practice simple anapana breath awareness (see pages 9–10) for a few minutes, as a stabilizing meditation.

2 Now imagine yourself vastly enlarged to the extent that you are sat on the bottom of a sea and the surface of the sea is level with your upper chest.

3 As you naturally inhale, imagine thousands of liters or gallons of water being sucked into you through a gateway located at the back of your lower spine, approximately level with your navel. This water fills your infinitely expandable lower belly. As you exhale, feel all that water being released through your belly, forming a powerful wave ahead of you.

4 With each inhalation draw in a greater quantity of water than before. With each exhalation, feel the wave ahead grow ever more powerful, until you can produce a vast tidal wave emanating from your belly. Spend a few breaths reducing the amount of water entering and leaving your lower spine, then a few further breaths increasing the volume again, until you have a sense of complete control over the movement of the sea.

5 Now think of any obstacle that you would like to overcome, or any situation that undermines you or makes you feel timid. Place that obstacle, or an image that encapsulates the situation, in the sea some distance in front of you.

6 Now, simply by focusing your breath in your belly and through your lower spine, visualize yourself mobilizing the full unstoppable power of the sea, to form a tide that can overwhelm any obstacle or situation that presents itself. (If the obstacle is another human being or group of human beings, imagine that the tide you have created moves them on to a situation even more favourable and pleasant for them. That way, you will not be using your will to undermine the fortunes of other people.)

7 Reflect that your lower body is in a continuum with the floor of the sea, preventing any chance of you being uprooted by the tides you have created. Your upper body has buoyancy in the water, which enables your spine to open, lengthen and therefore straighten. This relaxed uprightness imbues you with a confident demeanor, which further enhances your self-assurance.

Power affirmation

"My spine straightens and lengthens, as my back relaxes and chest opens. I have an ocean of resources to achieve my goals. I give that I may receive."

Water gives us power

Water covers the greater part of the world's surface, constantly eroding and depositing material from the land masses over aeons of time, reshaping whole continents in its stride. It has the power of life and death over the entire animal and plant kingdoms. None of the other natural elements of nature can harm water. It is true that fire can evaporate it, but that is the most temporary of transformations.

Water's characteristic of relentless power is reflected in human beings as the will power, confidence and self-assurance to stand our ground against all adversities and adversaries. It gives us the energy, the impetus and the will to continue in existence. If the metaphor of water is weak within us, we will lack self-confidence, resolve, and sufficient energy reserves. We will be unable to overcome inertia and we will be listless when it becomes necessary to take action. Rather than feeling like we have significant impact on the world, we will become timid and fearful.

FIRE AND LIGHT CONTEMPLATIONS

Another metaphor for consciousness is fire. All light is caused by fire in some form. In the natural universe, fire literally casts light and illuminates objects. Within human beings, fire is the metaphor for 'illumination' in that it gives us that 'spark' which is our raw consciousness; namely, that quality within us that can see and respond to those things that surround us. It could be argued that humanity's actual utilization of fire has played a significant role in its development of consciousness, by using the destructive and transforming quality of fire to control the environment, thus affording greater time to reflect on things rather than having to devote every waking minute to basic survival.

Light, and therefore fire, is in fact the universal symbol of consciousness, as expressed in such phrases as:

■ seeing the *light*
■ a *flash* of inspiration

Likewise, a very intelligent person is referred to as 'bright'. The very fact that we are able to visualize the images suggested in this book is dependent on the ability to create light and colour within our minds. Therefore, we must have a source of light within us, which is our consciousness.

If the metaphor of fire is weak within us, our inner light will not be as bright as it might be. We will find it difficult to visualize images with clarity, and appear to lack the sharpness of mind possessed by those who are really 'present'. This book is partly about visual imagery, so its usefulness depends on the level of light and colour that you, the reader, can generate in your mind.

The candle-gazing technique known as Trataka (see page 28) can be used as a good fire contemplation. The ancient yoga source books claim that this exercise can induce clairvoyance (meaning ultra-clarity of vision, unrestrained by linear time – hence we have another reference to light).

A great yogi called Patanjali describes, in his *Yoga Sutras*, a "Contemplation of the Inner Light." This meditation underlines the connection between light and consciousness. Here, Patanjali attempts to describe what is seen in the mind when one reaches an initial stage of enlightenment called samadhi:

In samadhi a great white light may be seen; the colourless light of pure consciousness. Sitting in a meditative posture, perfectly still, with eyes closed and senses withdrawn, the yogi may concentrate until perceiving a small point of light before the mind's eye. By concentrating the mind's energies on it, it will grow until he becomes filled with it and Super-consciousness occurs.

The following concentration and meditation exercise utilizes and enhances some of the qualities of fire within us.

Rising or setting sun contemplation

Gazing at the rising or setting sun is, in a way, literally 'treating fire with fire'. Watching the sun, or any form of fire, definitely clears away current mental dross, leaving space for greater clarity. Only do this exercise when the sun is sitting on the horizon, at dusk or dawn, and only if it is red. A red sun means that most of the ultraviolet light has been filtered out by the dust in the atmosphere. If it is rising or setting as a bright yellow sun, DO NOT STARE AT IT, or your mind's eye will be the only functioning eye that remains! Also, if you are in a valley, the sun will appear to set behind a horizon seemingly formed by the surrounding hills or mountains. This means that, although the sun is about to disappear from view, it is still at an angle of inclination that will damage your eyes. Thus, the rule is: the sun must be red and straight ahead. If you are in any doubt, do not do it.

1 Sit comfortably on a hill or seashore, as dawn is about to break or just before dusk. As the red sun rises or sets, look at it.
2 After a few seconds, close your eyes and dwell upon the imprint of the sun in your mind's eye. The image should appear as if it is literally imprinted on your forehead, between your eyebrows. For a while, immerse yourself in experiential feelings about warmth and light.
3 When it feels right, begin to contemplate the implications of the sun upon life or in relation to consciousness. Alternatively, you could visualize the imprinted sun image expanding to envelop and absorb your entire body. Then you can feel as one with the sun, imbibing its qualities of illumination, radiance and life-giving warmth.

IMAGERY AND SOUND VIBRATIONS FOR INTERNAL ORGANS

Sound is a very powerful tool for creating change, both physically (sonic weapons, for example) and in the psyche. Sound and music can evoke any emotions very quickly and effectively. If coupled with visual imagery, the effects are enhanced still further.

This chapter deals with visualizations and physical sound vibrations to benefit some of our internal organs. Later in this book, sound is explored in relation to mantras (see pages 106–129).

For the imagery part of the process, you will find that more than one color is offered for each organ. Try them and go with the color that feels right for you. Trust that you will intuitively select the colour most appropriate for your organ at that time, without needing to know any medical details about that organ. If you cannot seem to make up your mind, choose either color; it will be the right one. If you want to change the color at any time during the exercise, then do so, because that is also a natural and relevant part of this process. During some sessions you will want to stay with one color; at other times you will want to change colors.

For the sounds you make connected to these exercises, actually making them audible is best, because the resultant physical vibration has a strong effect on the relevant organ. However, you can also imagine the sound, which will still have a beneficial calming effect.

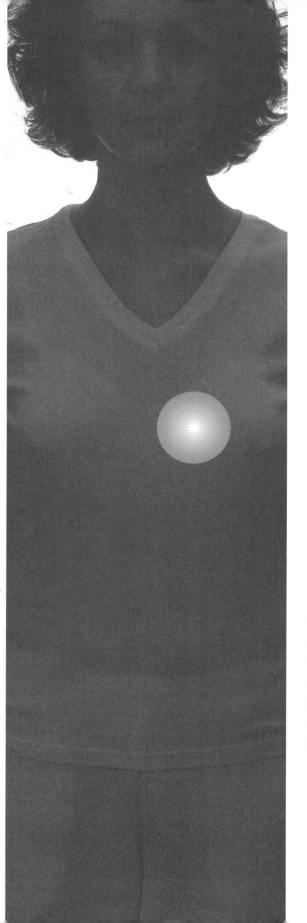

The heart

Your heart is located in the center of your chest cavity, behind your breastbone. Notice that the bottom half of the heart, which contains two main chambers known as ventricles, is angled downwards towards your left side. This means that the epicenter of your heart is slightly to the left side of your breastbone, which is where you will feel your heartbeat.

1 Sit in your preferred meditation position and place your left hand upon your breastbone, over your heart. Then place your right hand over your left hand.
2 Take two or three deep breaths, breathing in through your nose and out through your mouth. Feel through your palms the movement of your chest caused by your breathing.
3 During the next exhalation, which should be slow and drawn out for as long as is comfortable, sing the sound soooo (as in 'sooth') quietly to yourself. You will feel a gentle vibration under your left palm radiating into your heart. If you do not want to voice the sound aloud, imagine the sound permeating your heart as you breathe out.

The physical vibration from the physical sound soooo, or the more subtle vibration of the imagined sound, will automatically calm and harmonize your heart. If there is a problem with your heart and you want to heal it, do the exercise just described and simultaneously picture your heart either as a deep electric blue color or a deep red.

The lungs

Your lungs are located in your chest cavity, behind your ribs.

1   Sit in your preferred meditation position and cross your palms on your chest.

2   Take two or three deep breaths, breathing in through your nose and out through your mouth. Feel through your palms the movement of your chest caused by your breathing.

3   During the next exhalation, which should be slow and drawn out for as long as is comfortable, sing the sound aaaah quietly to yourself (or better still, loudly, if you can do so without embarrassment). As a result, you will feel a vibration under your palms radiating into your lungs. If you do not want to voice the sound aloud, imagine the sound permeating your lungs as you breathe out.

If there is a problem with your lungs and you want to heal them, do the exercise just described and simultaneously picture your lungs either as a bright, snow white color or as translucent with a silvery hue.

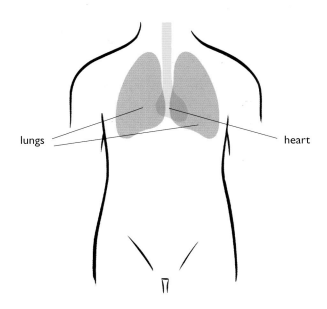

lungs   heart

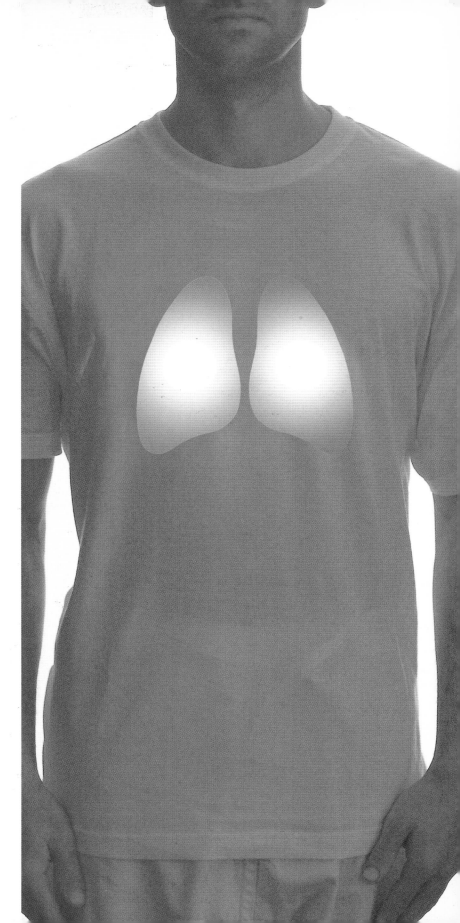

The kidneys

Your kidneys are ear-shaped organs about the size of your own fist and are located either side of your spine, in your right and left flanks. They are partly protected by the rear of your rib cage. Your kidneys are actually quite close to the surface of your body compared to other internal organs and, as such, are easily chilled if your flanks are left exposed.

1 Sit in your preferred meditation position and place your right hand over your right kidney and your left hand over your left kidney.
2 Take two or three deep breaths, breathing in through your nose and out through your mouth. Feel through your palms the movement of your flanks caused by your breathing.
3 During the next exhalation, which should be slow and drawn out for as long as is comfortable, sing the sound dooooe (as in bread 'dough') quietly to yourself, in as low a key as you can. As a result, you will feel a gentle vibration under your palms radiating into your kidneys. If you do not want to voice the sound aloud, imagine the sound permeating your kidneys as you breathe out.

The vibration from the physical sound dooooe, or the more subtle vibration of the imagined sound, will automatically calm and harmonize your kidneys. If there is a problem with your kidneys and you want to heal them, do the exercise just described and simultaneously picture your kidneys either as a shimmering, semi-translucent, silver color, a deep sea blue color or a deep maroon.

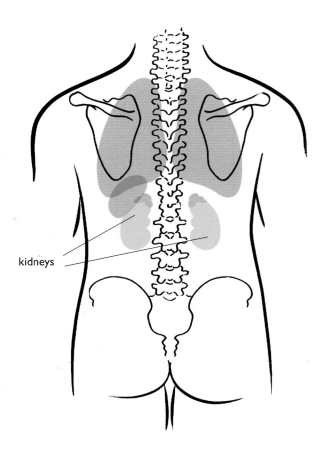

kidneys

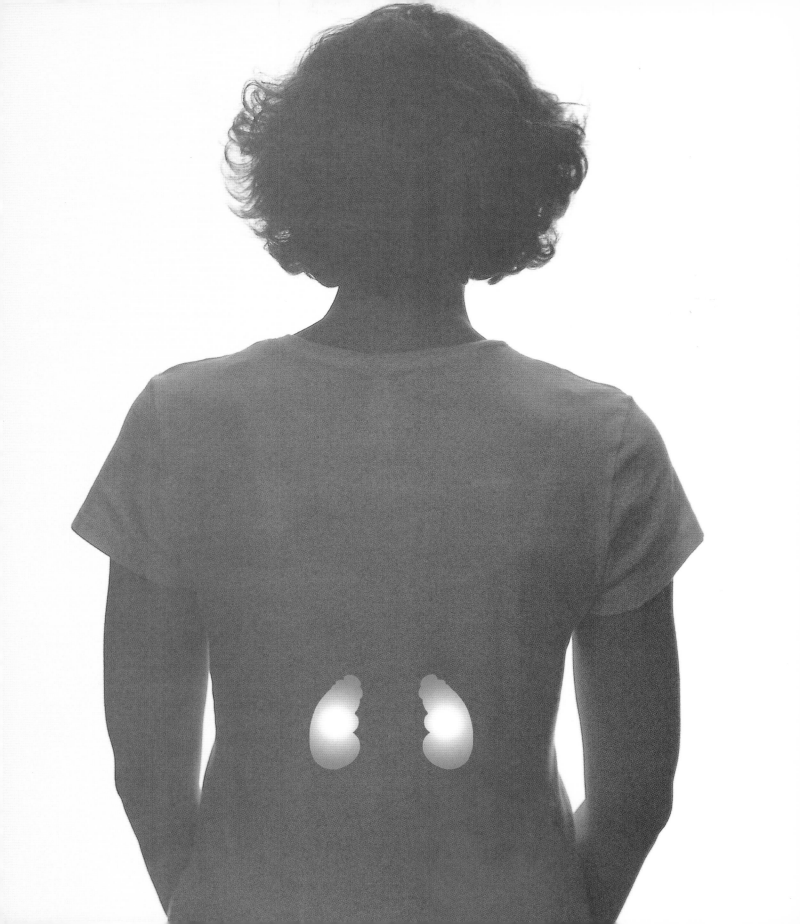

The liver

Your liver is located under your ribs on the right-hand side of your chest cavity.

1 Sit in your preferred meditation position and place your left hand upon your lower right ribs, over your liver. Then place your right hand over your left hand.
2 Take two or three deep breaths, breathing in through your nose and out through your mouth. Feel through your palms the movement of your ribs caused by your breathing.
3 During the next exhalation, which should be slow and drawn out for as long as is comfortable, sing the sound eeeee (as in 'bee') quietly to yourself. As a result, you will feel a gentle vibration under your left palm radiating into your liver. If you do not want to voice the sound aloud, imagine the sound permeating your liver as you breathe out.

The vibration from the physical sound eeeee, or the more subtle vibration of the imagined sound, will automatically calm and harmonize your liver. If there is a problem with your liver and you want to heal it, do the exercise just described and simultaneously picture your liver either as a bright, jade-like, aquamarine color or a deep maroon.

liver

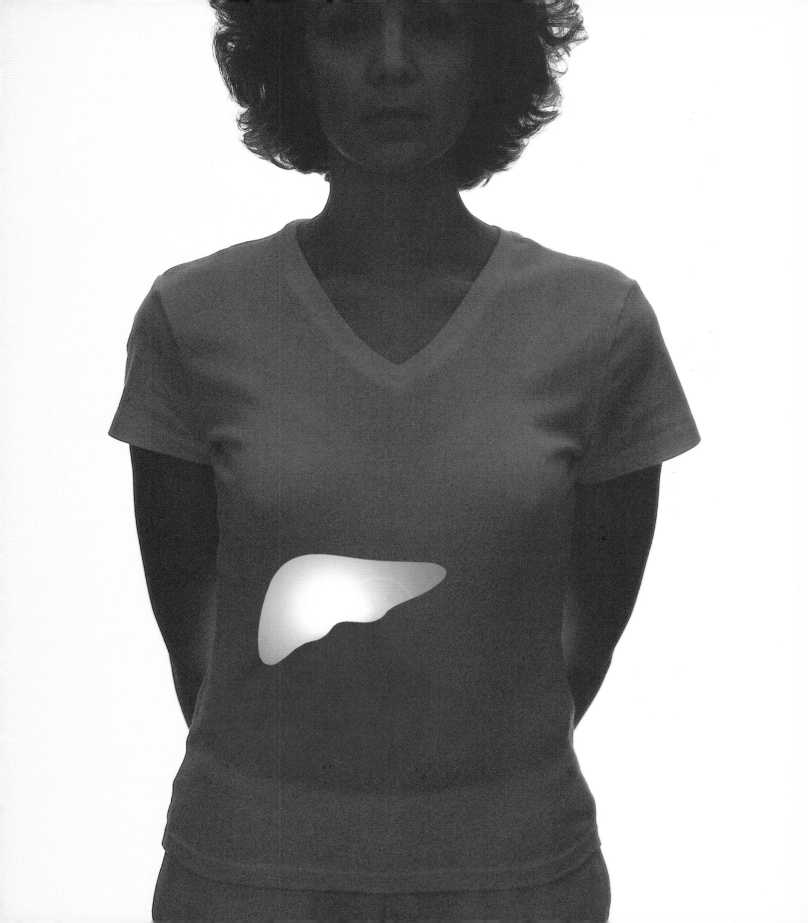

YOGA MEDITATION

This book explores meditation from various traditions, as well as exploring a number of its applications. However, many people in the western world have traditionally associated meditation with yoga, which is the context within which many people practice it. The word yoga means 'union' or 'identification', and comes from the same root as the verb 'to yoke'. In very general terms, the word yoga can be applied to any systematic method geared towards attaining 'union' or 'oneness' with true reality. It is particularly associated with the spiritual practices rooted in eastern philosophies. Thus, much of what has been discussed in this book so far can be placed within the practice of yoga.

However, the popular concept of yoga is of the practice of hatha yoga to gain control of the body, leading to raja yoga, to gain mastery of the mind. These aspects of yoga are just two of a number of paths to union, or enlightenment, which are practiced within the traditional philosophical frameworks of the Indian subcontinent. Most of these philosophies were developed by full-time meditators and sages known as

'Rishis'. There are six categories of Indian philosophy (seven if you include Buddhism, which is no longer practiced so much in India itself, but more so in adjoining countries). Yogic theory, as practiced today, stems mainly from two of the six philosophies: the *Yoga Sutras* of Patanjali, and *Vedanta* which is based on ancient texts known as the *Upanishads*. Patanjali's *Yoga Sutras* give detailed instructions for hatha and raja yoga, whilst *Vedanta* offers the philosophical backbone of jnana yoga, which is the yoga of using the intellect to enquire and contemplate. Yoga can also be connected to Buddhism, especially yoga tantra, which forms an aspect of the Tibetan Vajrayana Buddhist practice. However, much of what has been discovered and taught within yoga has been imported into other traditions, albeit often with some changes in terminology.

Yoga is a science of personal development. As stated earlier, it is incorporated into many eastern religions, but is equally valid within any world religion, or divorced from religion altogether. To quote a famous Indian yogi called Ramakrishna: "Through yoga a Hindu becomes a better Hindu, a Christian a better Christian, a Mohammedan a better Mohammedan, and a Jew a better Jew." The Hindu religion in particular borrows heavily from the classical Indian philosophies, therefore the iconography associated with the popular concept of yoga is common to Hinduism, especially in view of the fact that most Indian yoga gurus tend to be Hindus. As a result, the other sacred works of the Hindu, such as the *Bhagavad Gita*, have had a great influence on the shaping of yoga.

You may either be attracted or put off by an association of religion with your preferred meditation practice. As such, you can choose to take the whole package, religion and all, or you can cut through the cultural and religious accoutrements and extract the philosophical and practical essence of yoga to enrich your meditation practice.

The main yoga paths are classically listed as:

- **Raja yoga:** union by mental control, focusing on meditation and concentration
- **Karma yoga:** union by action, eliminating the ego and attachments through selfless service
- **Bhakti yoga:** union by devotion, through conversion of the emotions into devotion centered on the divine
- **Jnana yoga:** union by knowledge, using the intellect to break bondage to the material world

Of the above, bhakti yoga is most readily considered synonymous with religion, while both raja and jnana yoga are considered the most 'scientific'.

To the above list we can also add the following:

- **Hatha yoga:** an aspect of raja yoga, which works with the energies of the body and mind through exercises, postures and breathing methods
- **Mantra (japa) yoga:** union by sound, repeating special words, sentences and incantations to take the meditator to the essence and source of thought (this can be incorporated into raja and bhakti yoga)
- **Laya (latent) yoga:** a combination of most other yoga paths, with an emphasis on kundalini yoga, which is the systematic raising of energy upwards through the chakras as a rapid route to enlightenment

Most people who practice yoga incorporate many of the above paths at some level. Hence, in practice, the distinctions implied by the labeling are not so rigid. The purpose of this section within this book is to extrapolate some meditation principles from yoga. In practice, this means considering the methods employed within raja yoga, including mantra yoga.

The goal of yoga is to reach self-realization, which in Sanskrit is called samadhi. In the literature of yoga, the most systematic and useful book that describes the raja yoga path is the *Yoga Sutras*, written by Patanjali between 200 and 300 BCE. The second section of this classic book (as commented upon by many modern books on yoga) describes the disciplines designed to lead one progressively to samadhi. These disciplines are known as the eight limbs or angas of yoga. Their aim is to 'purify' the mind progressively so that the route to samadhi is smooth. Patanjali did not originally conceive these eight limbs; that happened much earlier in antiquity, but he was the first and most important codifier. The eight limbs (ashtanga) of yoga are:

- abstinences (*yamas*)
- observances (*niyamas*)
- postures (*asanas*)
- breath controls (*pranayama*)
- withdrawal of the senses (*pratyahara*)
- concentration (*dharana*)
- contemplation or meditation (*dhyana*)
- absorption or self-realization (*samadhi*)

The five abstinences (yamas)

These involve abstinence from killing and violence, falsehood, theft, damaging sexual behaviour and greed.

1 Non-violence (ahimsa)
This means extending compassion to all sentient creatures.

2 Truthfulness (satya)
This means not only abstaining from telling lies, but being sincere in all dealings with others. In other words, avoiding deceit at any level.

3 Non-stealing (asteya)
This includes abstinence from theft on all levels. It demands mindfulness of all your daily activities, to ensure that nothing is acquired, either materially or non-materially, by any means other than through the strict observance of fairness and honesty.

4 Chastity and continence (brahmacharya)
In a narrow sense, this means abstinence from the sexual act, so that the powerful sexual energy can be transmuted into the impetus for ultimately gaining enlightenment. This level of abstinence only really applies within a monastic situation. In ordinary life, it should be interpreted as restraint from a wasteful overindulgence in sexual activity, rather than a general judgement about the morals of sex.

5 Non-possessiveness (aparigrapha)
This can be translated as 'non-hoarding', but does not imply one should have no possessions. It means that we should not be enslaved by our possessions, or that their presence or the desire for them should not dominate our mind.

The five observances (niyamas)

The five observances are: purity, contentment, austerity, study, and attentiveness to higher principles.

1 Purity (saucha)
This includes specific methods to purge the body of poisons and to maintain hygiene. It includes advice about eating pure and appropriate foods. It is based on the idea that to purify the body helps to purify the mind.

2 Contentment (santosha)
This reminds us that meditation, whether or not practiced as an integral part of yoga, is accompanied by serenity of mind and greater harmony within ourselves and with our surroundings. Contentment is both a result of meditation and a psychological state that will help prevent us from being distracted during our meditation.

3 Austerity (tapas)
This term has often been mistaken to mean excessive asceticism or even deliberate self-inflicted mortification. It really refers to the application of sufficient self-discipline to achieve your goal, which in this context is samadhi. It is equivalent to the Buddhist 'middle way', which encourages the avoidance of extreme laziness on the one hand and extreme overexertion on the other.

4 Study (svadhyaya)
This has two aspects. One aspect is self-enquiry, leading to such questions as "who am I?" or "what am I?" to be addressed repeatedly until the ego is finally stripped away, leaving one's essential being exposed. The other aspect includes the mindful study of appropriate written material, which in the context of traditional Indian yoga would include classic texts such as the Upanishads. Buddhist yogis would study the Buddhist Sutras and Tantras, and yogis within other traditions would study the appropriate texts related to that tradition.

5 Attentiveness to higher consciousness (ishvara pranidhana)

This involves letting go of your ego's grip and placing trust in the validity of your spiritual practice. It is an invitation to stop clinging, and therefore to trust that all will work out better for you if you follow the path of mindfulness rather than the blind slavery of the ego and senses. For the more religiously inclined, this could mean 'giving oneself' or 'surrendering' to the Divine. For others, it can mean unconditionally trusting a guru or at least some higher principle.

These first two limbs (the yamas and niyamas) lay down guidance for the moral standards and conduct expected of a sincere seeker. They are not meant to delay the practice of meditation until one has developed a flawless morality, but offer a checklist to measure your higher personal growth and development. In other words, the list is not strictly hierarchical. It does not mean that you must first master the abstinences and observances before practicing the postures and then the breathing; all before specifically working on the mind. Instead, you should take note of the abstinences and observances and press on with your practice of meditation (and yoga asanas if you practice hatha yoga).

What is being said here is that the practice of meditation is much easier if you have your ethics and morals under control, because that makes for less distraction and guilt in life. But the practice of meditation will of itself cause you to reflect and be more aware of your conduct and interaction with others. As a result, your ethical and moral standards and practices will naturally be modified if you meditate regularly.

Limbs three and four are the postures (asanas) and the breath controls (pranayama) that belong to the practice of mastering the body, known as hatha yoga. This subject is covered within innumerable books. Since this book concerns methods of meditation, we will move on to limbs five to eight, although some aspects of pranayama are covered on pages 65–66, and an important, but limited, aspect of asanas has been addressed on pages 35–39, where seated meditation postures are discussed.

Withdrawal of the senses (pratyahara)

The fifth limb, pratyahara, involves the detachment of the mind from the sensory organs, in other words, shutting out the external world from our senses. To put it another way, it means the ability to wean one's thoughts from the endless fleeting sensations upon which they feed.

Pratyahara literally means 'gathering towards' or 'gathering in'. It is therefore the reigning in and integration of our scattered thoughts. We actually do this frequently without realizing it, as a means to stay subconsciously with our object of interest at any given time. For example, while we are fully absorbed in reading a book, we are not conscious of peripheral sounds such as the clock ticking. But when we stop reading the book and remain silent, it is then that we notice the ticking of the clock. Any form of intense concentration has the same effect. Lying in a sense deprivation tank would give you an experience of sense withdrawal. But what the yogi seeks through mastery of pratyahara is the conscious ability to sustain this withdrawal of the senses. There are many techniques to achieve this, but the methods of mindful one-pointed focus such as anapana (see pages 9–10) result in the mastery of pratyahara, and eventually the mastery of concentration (dharana).

Pratyahara is most clearly symbolized by the yoni mudra, whereby the mouth, nose and eyes are closed with the fingers, and the ears are blocked with the thumbs (see over). This serves to insulate the senses from distraction, thereby freeing the attention to dwell on the internal or mystic sounds called nadas, in particular, the sounds generated by the heart, known as anahata sounds.

The classic yoga text called the *Hatha Yoga Pradipika* metaphorically describes the quality of these internal mystic sounds, an extract of which is given here:

"In the beginning, the sounds that are heard are of great variety and very loud, but as the practice develops, they become increasingly subtle.

...Although one hears loud sounds like those of thunder and kettle drums, one should try to connect with the more subtle sounds only. If the mind wanders, alternate between connecting with the loud and the subtle sounds.

Wherever the mind first attaches itself, it becomes steady there, and then becomes absorbed there. Just as a bee, drinking sweet juice, does not care for the aroma of the flower; so the mind, absorbed in the nada, does not desire the object of enjoyment. The mind, like an elephant, habitually wandering in the garden of pleasure, is capable of being controlled by the sharp stimulus of anahata nada (heart sound). The mind, captivated in the snare of nada, surrenders all its activity, and, like a bird with clipped wings, immediately becomes calm."

Concentration (dharana)

Dharana is the sixth stage mentioned by Patanjali. It literally means concentration or complete attention. The mind exhibits its greatest power when focused on a single point rather than when scattered, in exactly the same way as the sun's rays can be collected and focused on a point of burning intensity through a magnifying glass. Most people spontaneously experience this intense focus from time to time. Do you remember an occasion when you were so focused on something that time had no meaning? At that time, did intuition and clear insight come streaming in, helping you to create what it was you were trying to do, be it finishing a painting or writing a masterful sentence? All flashes of inspiration undoubtedly manifest themselves out of this ultra-focused state. The purpose of practicing one-pointed attentiveness (dharana) is to gain conscious control of this ability, so that the power of the mind can be focused for more contemplative meditation practices.

In yoga, the mind is compared to the surface of a pool. If the surface of the pool is disturbed in any way, the bottom of the pool cannot be seen. Likewise, if the mind is agitated, we cannot fathom the depths of our mind. If we can hold the mind steady, on one subject or object, then we may catch a glimpse of our inner self; our raw and pure consciousness. Thus dharana is the bedrock of meditation insofar as it trains us to restrain the mind-stuff (chitta) from taking its habitual forms (vrittis). If you compare chitta to the surface of the pool, and vrittis to the thought-waves that cross it, then you should get the idea. Patanjali summed this up with the phrase "Yogas chitta vritti nirodha," which means "Yoga is the restraint of all mental distractions and modifications."

Any part of the body or any object can act as a focus for concentration. However, two favourites within raja yoga are energy centres called the 'ajna' chakra, also called the 'third eye', and the 'anahata' (heart) chakra. The ajna chakra is recommended for people of an intellectual inclination. The anahata chakra is recommended for those of a more emotional nature.

Pratyahara and dharana together equate to what we described earlier as stabilizing meditation (see page 14). Dharana is therefore a word that can describe the holding of an image in your mind's eye. Hence, the various visualization practices described throughout this book are examples of dharana. If you then contemplate the image, you are applying the next and seventh limb of yoga, which is dhyana.

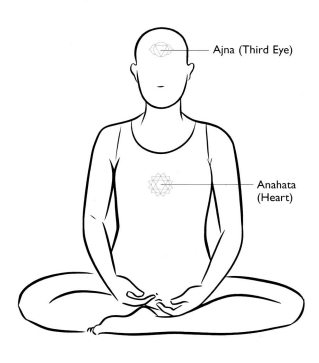

Ajna (Third Eye)

Anahata (Heart)

Contemplation or meditation (dhyana)

After mastery of concentration comes dhyana, which is equivalent to what was referred to earlier as analytical meditation or contemplation. Dharana can be summed up as the practice of holding an idea in the mind without the mind wavering from that idea.

In yoga, there are two types of analytical meditation:

Saguna: meditation with qualities. This refers to meditation upon something physically tangible and concrete such as a picture or some other external object.

Nirguna: meditation without qualities. This refers to meditation on an abstract idea or concept, such as love or consciousness itself.

Beginners should initially focus on saguna meditation, because it is easier than nirguna meditation. In saguna meditation, the object provides a solid point of reference. For example, if we take an apple as the object of meditation, its tangibility allows the mind to explore its shape, colour, aroma and uses systematically. In nirguna meditation, because there is no object to anchor the attention, the mind can easily wander down countless avenues, most of which will lead to a dead end. That is, until the mind is trained to go deep rather than go too broad.

In saguna meditation, the task is easier if the object is neutral, such as a rock or a spot on a wall, rather than something more subjective, such as your lover. This is because the former will have significantly less emotional attachment for you than the latter. However, the best object is something you consider to be a spiritual symbol, such as the Cross of Christ or a Buddha image. Such an image will lift your consciousness to a higher vibration rather than excite the lower, grasping nature of your mind.

In nirguna meditation, where the mind is fixed on an abstract idea, the mind will slowly 'melt', expand and become one with the formless abstract idea itself. This is less likely to happen during the more concrete saguna method.

A good example of a traditional nirguna meditation is one known as 'Contemplation of the void', as described in the classic text on yoga called the *Siva Samhita*:

"Let him [the yogi] contemplate his own reflection in the sky .... Through that, let him think on the Great Void unceasingly. The Great Void, whose beginning is void, whose middle is void, whose end is void, has [the] brilliancy of tens of millions of suns, and the coolness of tens of millions of moons. By contemplating continually on this, one obtains success. Let him practice daily, with energy, this dhyana. Within a year he shall undoubtedly obtain all success. He whose mind is absorbed in that place, even for a second, is certainly a yogi, and a good devotee, and is revered in all worlds. All his stores of sins are at once verily destroyed. By seeing it, one never returns to the path of this mortal universe ...."

Absorption or self-realization (samadhi)

The end result of mastering concentration (dharana) and meditation (dhyana) is a natural absorption into the eighth limb, known as self-realization (samadhi), a state where the contemplated object or subject becomes one with our consciousness. It is a state of pure existence, where the ego ceases to exist. All sense of 'I' and 'mine' evaporates. It is transcendence beyond worries, fears, desires and attachments. Obviously such a state cannot be adequately described to us, because samadhi is a state of being that is totally beyond our experience. It must be like trying to describe the concept of deep space to a duck. In yoga, the experience is summed up with the phrase sat-chit-ananda, which means 'being' (sat) – 'consciousness' (chit) – 'bliss' (ananda). Spiritual literature is full of attempts to describe the indescribable. Some of the clearer and concise attempts to describe samadhi are as follows.

Swami Vishnu Devananda said in his book *Meditation and Mantras*: "There is neither darkness nor void; all is light. Dualities vanish. There is neither subject nor object. There is neither meditation nor samadhi. There is neither meditator nor the meditated upon. There is neither pleasure nor pain. There is only perfect peace and absolute bliss."

A yogi called Ramana Maharshi described samadhi as "remaining in the primal, pure, natural state without effort." He also said: "Once attained, the state of self-realization is the same by whatever path and through whatever religion it may be approached."

Samadhi is not a sudden bursting into a single level of total awareness. It has several stages, the fine details of which are perhaps unnecessary to know unless one has been there. However, two important stages of samadhi were described by the yogi Vivekananda. These stages he labeled 'with seed' and 'without seed'. If we return to the idea that our mind is like a pool and our thoughts are the waves on its surface, then, according to Vivekananda:

■ concentration (dharana) reduces the waves to a single point
■ meditation (dhyana) maintains that point for some time
■ samadhi 'with seed' replaces the wave with singular awareness of the controlling thought
■ samadhi 'without seed' arises when identification with the controlling thought itself fades away.

The ultimate 'without seed' stage of self-realization is called nirvikalpa samadhi. It is a state of complete dissolution of any identification with 'self.'

It is characterized by immeasurable bliss, free from confusion, because there is no separation of the self from totality, or universal consciousness, to be confused.

For the sake of simplicity and clarity, concentration is usually described as a preliminary requisite for meditation, which itself is something to be mastered in order to reach self-realization. In other words, it appears to be a vertical methodology with samadhi as the goal. However, many yogis have elaborated on this and confirm that one moves up and down this ladder between samadhi and ordinary consciousness, rather than automatically remaining in samadhi once it has been attained. In fact, the first time a samadhi state is achieved, it may only last for a few seconds. By continuing to meditate, the ability to remain in samadhi for longer increases. However, even when one can naturally remain in samadhi for extended periods of time, it is still necessary to practice concentration and meditation to maintain that ability.

It is tempting to be impatient for the experience of samadhi, or super-consciousness, but samadhi is the result of a long-term, dedicated process. In the meantime, if you meditate regularly, you will become more poised, have brighter eyes, exude greater calmness and generally become a lot more tolerant. It is definitely worth it.

WHAT IS A MANTRA?

The practice of reciting mantras is very widespread within many spiritual traditions, including Christianity, Sufism, Buddhism and Hinduism. It involves the repetition of a word or series of words that are selected either because:

- the word's literal meaning reminds us of some higher spiritual principle,
  or
- the vibration evoked by the sound has an inherent power, which may be independent of the literal meaning of the sound, if indeed it has one.

In eastern spiritual disciplines, the use of mantras is called japa or mantra meditation, a mantra being a combination of sounds derived from the Sanskrit alphabet. The word 'mantra' is a Sanskrit word which literally means 'that which protects and purifies the mind'. This type of practice is based on very precise cosmological theories within traditional Indian philosophies. Interestingly, these theories bear close resemblance to modern quantum physics. According to these yogic theories, sound is the substratum of the cosmos and the key factor in causing the cosmos to manifest itself. A broad overview of this yogic cosmological view is as follows.

The latent, formless universe, that is, before it has actually manifested itself, is known as shakti. Thus, shakti is a term for what is often called the 'absolute' or the 'void.' The material universe manifests itself out of shakti, which means shakti 'gives birth' to the universe. Giving birth is an essentially female principle, so that is why shakti is seen as a female energy.

Latent within shakti are the three primal qualities of the universe, or 'trigunas,' known as purity (sattva), activity (rajas), and inertia (tamas). The latency of shakti is disturbed by a great cosmic vibration that splits shakti into two polarized forces known as nada and bindu. Together, these two forces become the substratum of the cosmos, providing the magnetic force to hold the molecules of the physical world together, yet in a state of vibration.

Nada is the centripetal, female energy. Because it is centripetal, it is the substratum that ultimately condenses into the wavelengths of audible sound and ultimately into matter. Therefore, nada could be thought of as 'the power of becoming.' It equates to yin in the Daoist cosmological view. Nada literally means 'sound,' and within the context of yoga it means 'inner mystic sound' because, through meditation and mantra, it is possible to tune into this substratum through sound.

Bindu is considered to be the centrifugal, male energy. As such, bindu can be considered the latent energy that motivates nada. As an analogy, this is rather like the relationship between a sound wave itself (equating to nada) and the energy that propels the wave (bindu). Bindu equates to yang in Daoist cosmology. Bindu and nada are really aspects of the same phenomenon, and cannot truly be separated. The word 'bindu' literally means 'dot' or 'mark.' According to the Cologne Sanskrit dictionary, it can mean 'sudden development out of one drop'. A good example of this is the sudden expansion of oil when it comes into contact with the surface of water. In the cosmological context, nada, the manifested sound wave, is analogous to the expanding oil. Bindu is the means

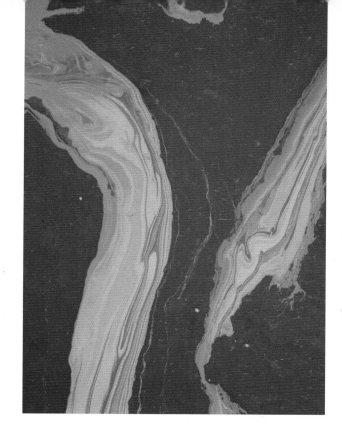

by which the sound wave is carried out of the 'empty' void, and is analogous to the energy of the expanding oil.

After this initial polarizing (but not separating) of energies into bindu and nada, the resultant vibrating energies of the universe continue to expand and divide into a variety of wavelengths. It is said that after the fifth stage of division (of nada, propelled by bindu), these energies manifest themselves on the gross plane, revealing themselves to us as color and sound. Later in this book, I present the theory of Daoist meditation. What is interesting is that we can see a very close parallel between the traditional Chinese (Daoist) cosmological view and that of ancient India. The 'manifestation of the universe' story is almost identical, separated only by the semantics of each tradition. For example, the great Daoist philosopher Lao Zi, who is considered to be the creator of Daoism, wrote: "The Dao begot one. One begot two. Two begot three, and three begot 10,000 things."

अ आ र क ख ग घ ङ ह क्ष

इ ई ए च छ ज झ ञ य श ज्ञ

ऋ ॠ ओ ट ठ ड ढ ण र ष

ल ॡ औ त थ द ध न ल स त्र

उ ऊ औ प फ ब म व

50 root syllables of Sanskrit

After the fifth stage of division (of nada, propelled by bindu), fifty articulate sounds are created, each one corresponding to one of the fifty root syllables of Sanskrit, known as varnas. Interestingly, 'varna' actually means color, so this gives us an insight into why all sound vibrations have a corresponding color vibration. Combinations of these fifty primeval sounds give rise to all forms that manifest themselves in the physical world. Therefore, we can say that all sound has potential form, and all form has a corresponding sound.

Mantras then, are words and sounds based on the fifty Sanskrit syllables, which themselves directly equate to the raw universal sounds known as varnas. Note that mantra syllables have power whether they are repeated vocally or mentally.

Japa meditation is usually practiced for the purpose of connecting with, or evoking, the qualities of a selected deity. The selected deity always embodies the spiritual qualities to which the meditator aspires. In other words, the deity represents a being with more developed attributes than oneself, and the meditator aspires to be like that deity. As such, japa meditation is primarily an aspect of bhakti yoga, a devotional practice, with a choice of two nuances: one religious and one non-theistic. It is also a strong component of yoga tantra and Tibetan Vajrayana Buddhism insofar as the tantric yogi is trained to think and behave like a particular enlightened being, so that through total affirmation and guided esoteric practices, the yogi eventually becomes an enlightened being. Put another way, rather than aspiring to be enlightened and climbing a 'hill' to reach the goal, the practitioner of tantra habitually acts as if he or she is already on top of the hill. So whereas the non-tantric aspirants progressively claw their way uphill, the tantric Vajrayana practitioners are forever vigilant not to slip downhill.

In the religious nuance, devotion means the surrender of oneself to the concept of a god, who is seen as an actual entity. For example, if a Hindu repeats the mantra 'OM Namah Sivaya' with sufficient devotion, he or she will evoke a remembrance of Lord Siva, the Hindu god responsible for destroying one's lower nature to make way for the development of higher attributes. The devout Hindu will wish ultimately to connect with Lord Siva himself, to receive blessings and guidance towards the goal of self-realization.

To the non-Hindu, repetition of 'OM Namah Sivaya' still means attuning oneself to the qualities needed to help destroy one's lower nature. These qualities are inherent within the sound vibration of the mantra, irrespective of whether the image of Lord Siva is held or not. The non-theist may still evoke the image of Siva through the verbal or mental repetition of the mantra, but see it as a purely symbolic metaphor for those qualities. However, it is generally accepted that the addition of the relevant deity image adds to the power of the mantra.

Effects of mantra within the human being

Most eastern philosophies have based their understanding of the human being on the idea that the individual is a reflection of the cosmos in miniature. We therefore have the expression that a human being is 'a microcosm of the macrocosm'. For example, the cosmic cycles of expansion and contraction reflect in humankind as the rhythm of the breath and in the beating of the heart. Another example is the alternating manifestation and dissolution of things, both macrocosmically and microcosmically. For instance, planets, stars and galaxies are born, grow and decay, a pattern reflected by all sentient beings.

In humans, nada, the centripetal 'manifesting/becoming' power of the universe, takes form as a latent force called kundalini that can be metaphorically thought of as an energy lying coiled and dormant at the base of the spine, rather like a sleeping

serpent. The kundalini is the sum total of the fifty basic sounds in their pre-manifest state, much like shakti is a pre-manifestation of sound at the macrocosmic level. Hence, kundalini is sometimes called kundalini shakti. Another way of expressing this concept is that, latent within the kundalini, the fifty basic sound wavelengths are awaiting expression. It is because of kundalini that we have the ability to produce a gross articulation of these fifty sounds through our vocal chords.

Remember that our head and torso is mostly hollow and will thus resonate like an instrument. Also, it is largely composed of water, which is an excellent sound conductor. It follows therefore that, if we can vocalize sounds, especially ones that precisely match

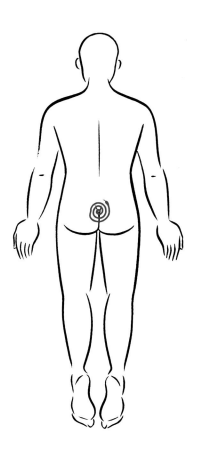

one or more of the fifty primal sounds, then the kundalini can be affected by those vocalized sounds. If the method is selected and understood with sufficient skill, the kundalini energy may be aroused and directed as a force for the rapid expansion of consciousness. On the other hand, if it is aroused without sufficient skill to control it, then it could create problems such as serious physical and mental disturbances. That is why such practices are traditionally only passed on and supervised by those who have successfully completed the process themselves.

Earlier I mentioned that a mantra can be repeated mentally rather than verbally and still retain much of its effectiveness. This is because traditional yogic theory and physics both consider thought, physical form and sound to be different aspects of the same oscillating energy. That might seem remarkable, but as an exercise (make it a contemplative meditation if you like), consider the different attributes of water, ice and steam. These attributes are completely different from each other, yet they are the same substance. Now imagine having no life experience to know that they are they same, which is equivalent to the oneness of thought, form and sound seeming remarkable. Through such contemplations, one can see that many esoteric notions may hold true.

So if thought, sound and form are one and the same, it must follow that:

■ thinking a sound or vocalizing that sound can produce a specific mental image
■ by meditating on a physical form, image or abstract concept, it may be possible to discern the 'sound' of that image or concept
■ by making or thinking a sound whilst visualizing a form, any associated ideas, qualities, emotions and other attributes of the combined sound and image may be revealed

This is why, if the word 'Siva' is held in the mind or heard through the ears, the form of Siva manifests itself in the consciousness. Likewise, if a Siva mantra is repeated enough times, one's negative traits may dissolve, because the wavelength for destroying negative traits has the same wavelength as the sound and image of Siva.

Language gives us a tapestry of words associated with images, which in turn evoke emotions. For example, if you are swimming in the sea and someone next to you says "shark," the image of a shark will immediately occur in your mind and the emotions of fear and panic will immediately be felt, even if there is no shark. Another person who does not understand your language may be nearby and also hear the word "shark." Assuming there is no panic in the intonation, he or she will experience no fear. In that person's language, "shark" might mean "look at that gorgeous body," which will almost certainly lead to other images and emotions.

Normal language, then, represents the concrete end of the spectrum, and depends upon a learned understanding of the words. On the other hand, mantras pronounced correctly, and based on the fifty Sanskrit syllables, represent a raw vibration that can evoke specific images, thoughts and emotions independent of any literal understanding. Japa, using tried and tested mantras, purges the mind of attachment to anger, greed, self-pity and any other emotion that may obstruct your quest for higher consciousness. Japa simply causes your thoughts to vibrate at a higher level. If a deity mantra is repeated with genuine devotion, the virtues and power of that deity permeate the aspirant's mind, ultimately allowing the real possibility for self-realization (samadhi). If the aspirant has knowledge of the meaning of the mantra and of the attributes of the deity, then illumination will come relatively quickly. If there is no knowledge of the meaning, the raw vibratory energy of the mantra will also bring illumination, albeit more slowly.

Once chosen, or given to you by a guru, your deity mantra should not be changed. The more one-pointed the focus when japa is practiced, the deeper and quicker the effect. The effect is cumulative, so you need to keep it up every day. It is best to practice it within a formal meditation 'sitting,' in addition to doing it during regular daily activity, when the mind is not otherwise usefully occupied. You will be amazed how much time can accumulate.

Traditional yogic texts describe the eventual culmination of japa as an upward rush of energy that exits from the top of the head. This energy then rains down over the body, bathing it with a feeling of soft electricity.

Saguna and nirguna mantras

Mantras that have a clear image associated with them are called saguna mantras. They are always connected to the image and qualities of a deity, or a symbol relating to a deity. With continual repetition of the mantra, the form of the deity or symbol manifests itself as the visual component of the sound vibration. The aim is to feel as if the deity has actually manifested before you, or to experience yourself dissolving into oneness with that deity.

Mantras that have no deities, and no specific form at all, in other words abstract mantras, are called nirguna mantras. Nirguna mantras are particularly appropriate for those people who are not drawn to a personal deity, those who see the universe as an interplay of interconnecting energies. This type of mantra will suit you if you wish to identify with the cosmic substrata in general and as a whole. As such, nirguna mantras tend to be for those people inclining towards the non-theistic, while saguna mantras are for people of a more theistic inclination.

'OM' is considered to be the supreme mantra, representing the sum total of all sounds within the universe. It has been described as the underlying sound of the cosmic substrata. Furthermore, it is considered to be the sound vibration that caused the universe to come into being. OM is therefore the root of all mantras, all sounds and ultimately of all things.

OM is recognized in many cultures as being the most complete and universal sound. To the Mayans, the O of OM is linked with both higher consciousness and the heavens, and the M is linked with the earth. The Latin word 'omnes,' which means 'all' or 'everything,' is another example. The Hindus say that the universe comes from OM, rests in OM and dissolves in OM.

In japa yoga theory, the correct pronunciation of a mantra is critical to achieve its maximum impact. Therefore OM is more correctly pronounced AUM. The sound A (Ah) emanates deep within your belly, but can be clearly felt in the region of your heart. U (Ouh) progresses upwards to your throat, and M (MMM) continues upwards to the top of your head. Try it. Place one hand on the center of your chest and the other on top of your head; slowly chant AUM and you will feel the A – U – M clearly vibrate in your chest, throat and head respectively. This has

great significance, as the following few paragraphs will explain.

The universe works according to polarity, meaning that opposites attract in an attempt to return to oneness. Maleness attracting femaleness is one example of this. The ancient Chinese saw this in the observation that humans exist as a receptacle through which the forces of earth meld with the forces of the heavens (see page 152). For example, they saw that maleness is centrifugal. It has the predominant attributes of outwardness, meaning that male strength (muscular strength) is on the exterior and his genitals are on the outside. He subdues his physical environment through conquest of one sort or another, by utilizing his greater muscular strength and aggressiveness. He sees the world in a very physical way, yet he is aware of something beyond the physical, beyond his understanding. Through the law of polarity, of magnetism, he may be

drawn to deep cogitation about the nature of the universe, of consciousness and a whole spectrum of philosophical questions. Hence, it is maleness that yearns for the unanswerable solutions to mystical questions. In other words, man is expanding outwards from the physical, reaching towards the ethereal.

Femaleness is centripetal. It has the predominant attributes of drawing inwards, meaning that female strength is on the interior (stamina) and her genitals are on the inside. Like magnetism, her centripetal energy attracts the expansive centrifugal energy. Thus, she naturally fills with the expansiveness of the heavens. She intuitively understands her connection with cosmic influences. No doubt that is why women are considered to be more intuitive, and why more women appear to have more clairvoyant tendencies compared to men.

The modern reader may consider what was just said as incongruous with modern attitudes to gender equality. Firstly, this is the ancient Chinese and Indian yogic view rather than a personal opinion. Secondly, it is maleness and femaleness that are being compared rather than males and females. This view recognizes that all males have femaleness within them and all females have maleness within them.

So what has this got to do with OM or AUM? In yogic theory, *A* represents the physical plane because it resonates in the lower cavities of the body, which are closer to the earth and contain the organs pertaining to more animalistic functions, such as reproduction and digestion. However, because *A* represents the physical, through the law of attraction it attunes with the immaterial, the heavens. Thus, when the Mayans say that *O* or *A* is linked with higher consciousness and yogic theory states that *A* represents the physical plane, one can begin to understand this seeming paradox.

In yoga, *U* represents the mental and astral planes, and *M* corresponds to everything beyond the understanding of the intellect. Again, we have the apparent contradiction between the Mayan and Indian interpretation. To the Mayans, *M* relates to the earth. This makes sense, because it has a centripetal quality that brings things into being, exemplified in words such as 'manifest', materialize' and 'make'. In yoga, *M* relates to higher consciousness, because it resonates in our head, which contains our higher senses. However, that centrifugal energy attracts its opposite, hence we can use our intelligence and intuition to make sense of, and manipulate, the physical world.

Some other relationships that resonate with the pronunciation of AUM are:

A	U	M	A-U-M COMBINED
waking state	dreaming state	deep sleep state	samadhi
speech	mind	breath (prana)	individual living spirit
length	breadth	depth	beyond shape and form
absence of desire	absence of fear	absence of anger	perfect being
past	present	future	transcendence of time

The significance of the items on this list may not be immediately obvious, but I include them because their interrelationships can be a useful focus for contemplation (analytical meditation).

Repetition of the mantra OM will resonate in every cell of your body, right down to the atomic level. Extensive repetition over time will awaken dormant physical and mental capacities. So you might well think that because OM is so universal and inclusive, why bother with any other sound? The limitation of OM as a mantra is that it is completely abstract, so its lack of form makes it difficult to incorporate any imagery or concept. However, it has tremendous power based on its sound vibration alone, so if you have not chosen or been given another mantra, you can use OM until such time as you find a more specific one.

Bija or 'seed' mantras are powerful, single-syllable sounds derived from the fifty primeval sounds. They have no literal meaning but each resonates with an abstract metaphysical concept or with an element of nature. For example, each of the universal elements has a particular bija that resonates with it:

Ether	=	HAM
Air	=	YAM
Fire	=	RAM
Water	=	VAM
Earth	=	LAM

Within Hinduism and traditional Indian philosophies such as Vedanta, a bija syllable has also been identified for each deity. However, the general practice of performing japa exclusively upon any seed syllable is considered fruitless unless one has achieved a state where the very abstract nature of the cosmos is perceived. Therefore, only very advanced yogis would find any benefit in doing that. Instead, bija syllables are incorporated in more diverse multisyllable mantras to lend them power and provide a direct link to the cosmic substrata. They act as a kind of 'seed' that is implanted in the mind, ready to germinate into a catalyst to help rid ourselves

of any traits that will impede our spiritual progress. In other words, they mostly lie dormant until a level of spiritual unfoldment is about to occur, at which time the power of the bija (seed) syllable is released. The abstract (nirguna) mantras given next are examples of mantras that contain one or more bija syllables.

Abstract mantras

SOHAM (SO-HUHMM)
I am that I am

This mantra consists of two bija syllables: SO and HAM. SO resonates with the centripetal female energy (nada), and HAM resonates with the expansive male energy (bindu). Consequently, it is considered a powerful catalyst for unifying one's individual consciousness with the universal consciousness. This mantra is commonly practiced within the Hindu and Buddhist traditions as an accompaniment to meditating on the breath. It is repeated mentally as follows:

SO with the in-breath
HAM with the out-breath

The main polarities represented by SO and HAM are listed above.

SO	HAM
Female energy	**Male energy**
Inward	**Outward**
Nada (yin)	**Bindu (yang)**
Inhalation	**Exhalation**
Cold	**Hot**

Remember that one object of the mantra is to integrate the qualities of SO and HAM to create a better balance within your mind, body and spirit. Therefore, if you are too cold or too hot, the mantra will help create a more neutral temperature. If your personality is excessively introvert or extrovert, the mantra will encourage a more serene and charismatic demeanor. Ultimately, this mantra is designed to slow the pendulum of consciousness from swinging wildly between nada and bindu, between past and future, so that the meditator becomes existence itself, without form, qualities or limitations.

To say the mantra aloud, with the SO on the in-breath, takes some skill. Inhale through the mouth, allowing the air to pass between your teeth and over your tongue, to create a hissing SSS sound. At this point you will clearly experience the cooling effect in your mouth. As you then further relax your jaw, the OH sound will manifest in the throat. As you exhale, you whisper HAH, slowly closing your lips to create a silent MM. The mantra should be vocalized very quietly, audible only to yourself and perhaps anyone immediately next to you. SO and HAM should ideally be of equal duration.

TAT TWAM ASI (the _W_ is pronounced as a cross between _V_ and _W_)
That thou art

TAT (That) resonates with the creative force of the cosmos, the universal 'Oneness' or substrata that is creation itself. Vedantic philosophy calls this creative force, 'brahman.' TWAM (Thou) is the meditator. Therefore this meditation identifies the individual as indistinguishable from the cosmic substrata, resulting in a mantra that acts as an effective dissolver of the ego.

OM MANI PADME HUM (AUM MAH-NEE PAHD-MAY HOOM)
Hail, the jewel in the lotus

This is a universal mantra within Buddhism. The OM at the beginning resonates with the universal inclusiveness of all things. The HUM at the end resonates with that part of the whole that is you, the meditator. MANI literally means jewel, which is a metaphor for your higher consciousness or spirit that is capable of compassion.

Your higher consciousness is considered to reside in your heart, which is metaphorically depicted as a lotus, hence the word PADME, which means lotus.

Essentially, this mantra causes a powerful vibration that has the power to resonate with, and therefore awaken, a greater potential for compassion within you. It is also commonly used as a Tibetan Buddhist deity (saguna) mantra, in which case, the Buddha of Compassion (called Avalokiteshvara) is simultaneously visualized. Note that in Tibetan Buddhism, the last syllable HUM is usually pronounced HUNG (HOONG).

OM AH HUM
Enter into me, O Universal sound of OM

This mantra consists of three bija syllables representing the three stages of the cosmic cycle: becoming, maintaining and dissolving. In humans and all other living things, these equate to birth, life and death. As such, this is a good abstract mantra that attunes well with contemplations on the nature of impermanence or of time. The first and last syllables, OM and HUM, are best held for three times the length of the middle syllable AH.

DEITY MANTRAS

This section gives examples of classic deity mantras from the traditional philosophies of India, and the Hindu and Buddhist traditions, which contain a prolific supply of such mantras, and are based directly on Sanskrit syllables. In addition, there are examples from other traditions.

Deity mantras from traditional Indian lineages

OM NAMAH SIVAYA (the S in Sivaya has a hint of SH in the pronunciation)
Prostrations to Lord Siva

In the Hindu religion there is a trinity of deities: Brahma the creator, Vishnu the preserver and Siva the destroyer. Siva is known as the Cosmic Dancer, and embodies the forces of destruction that dissolve the universe at the end of each age. Hence, mantras containing Siva attune with the process where the old gives way to the new. In us, the power of Siva (both the raw sound vibration of Siva and the embodiment of Siva as a deity) encourages the destruction of our lower nature, so that positive spiritual growth may occur.

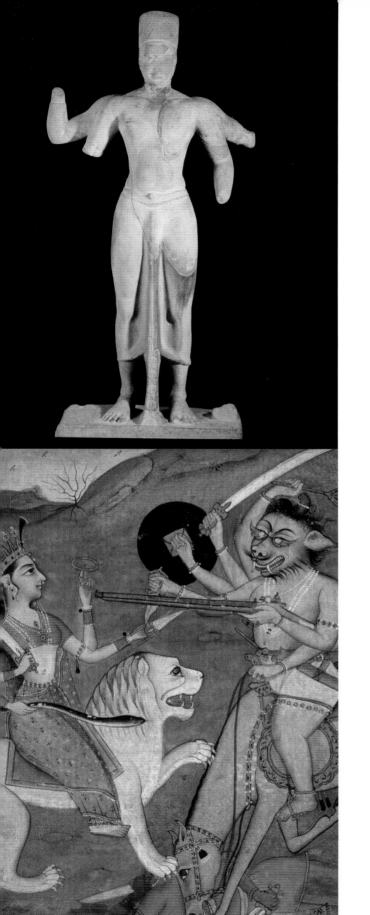

OM NAMO NARAYANAYA
Prostrations to Lord Vishnu

ॐ नमो नारायणाय ।

The sounds of both NARAYANA and VISHNU resonate with the principle of preservation. In Hinduism, Narayana is another name for Lord Vishnu, the deity who preserves order and harmony in the world. This mantra is therefore a good one for people wishing to develop more harmony in their lives, or in the world through their work.

OM SRI DURGAYAI NAMAH (SRI is pronounced SHREE. The UR in DURGA has a slight OOR nuance in pronunciation)
Prostrations to Mother Durga

ॐ श्रीदुर्गायै नमः ।

Sri is a title of reverent respect. Durga represents the female aspect of the cosmos, or to the Hindu, the motherhood aspect of God. She is the deity manifestation of shakti, the force that manifests the universe. Therefore, Durga represents latent power, like the ocean. Like a good mother, she is seen as a benefactor and protector. Durga therefore represents the concept of shakti in deity allegory, as stated in Hindu mythology, where it is said that the pure consciousness of Brahma (creation), Siva (destruction) and Vishnu (preservation) united to form Durga (the 'mother' aspect of the universe).

HARE RAMA HARE RAMA, RAMA RAMA HARE HARE; HARE KRISHNA, HARE KRISHNA, KRISHNA KRISHNA HARE HARE

My Lord Rama! My Lord Krishna!

हरे राम हरे राम राम राम
हरे हरे। हरे कृष्ण हरे कृष्ण
कृष्ण कृष्ण हरे हर।

In Hindu bhakti yoga, this is the Maha Mantra, or supreme mantra for the purpose of attaining liberation in this age. Rama and Krishna were incarnations of Vishnu. Rama is the embodiment of righteousness and virtue. He represents the ideal husband and son, and is thus particularly applicable to those with family responsibilities. Krishna is one of the most well known deities of India, being the main figure in the key yoga text, the *Bhagavad Gita*. He is very playful, generous and extrovert, and appeals to people who are concerned for the welfare of others. The word 'hare' is an invocation designed to attract the attention of the deities, much like 'hail' or 'here!'

OM TRAYAMBAKAM YAJAMAHE SUGUNDHIM PUSHTI-VARDHANAM URVARUKAMIVA BANDHANAN MRITYOR MUKSHIYA MAMRITAT

We worship the three-eyed Lord [Siva] who is full of sweet fragrance and nourishes human beings. May he liberate me from bondage, even as a cucumber is severed from the vine.

ॐ त्र्यम्बकं यजामहे सुगन्धिं
पुष्टिवर्धनम् उर्वारुकमिव
बन्धनान् मृत्योर् मुक्षीय मामृतात

As well as having the impetus to lead one to self-realization, this mantra is said to remove all diseases and prevent accidents (if repeated extensively every day). It is referred to as the Maha Mrityunjaya mantra.

Deity mantras from Buddhist lineages

In the Theravadan Buddhist lineages, only the energy of Shakyamuni Buddha would be incorporated into a deity mantra, because there are no other deities in Theravadan Buddhism. The Mahayana Buddhist traditions incorporate other Buddhas and Bodhisattvas (Bodhisattvas are highly advanced spiritual aspirants who have chosen to postpone supreme Buddhahood until all beings have reached enlightenment), but it is the Mahayana and Vajrayana paths of Tibetan Buddhism in particular that emphasize the use of deity mantras. The examples given below are from the Tibetan traditions, where visualization practices in relation to deity mantras are particularly developed. Note that it is customary in Buddhism to dedicate the positive energy and insight gained from the practice towards the benefit and future enlightenment of all beings.

OM MUNI MUNI MAHA MUNAYE SOHA
The mantra of Shakyamuni Buddha

ॐ मुनि मुनि महामुनये स्वाहा।

Shakyamuni Buddha refers to the historical Buddha who is believed to have lived during the 5th and 6th centuries BCE. He is the fourth of the 1,000 Buddhas who are predicted to appear within the current aeon. The next Buddha will be the Buddha Maitreya.

This mantra is a powerful deity mantra, made more so by the following visualization, which has been simplified for beginners (although there is still tremendous power in the mantra without the visualization):

1 Visualize Shakyamuni Buddha (see below) about 1.8 metres/6 feet in front of your forehead. Visualize rays of light emanating from each pore of the Buddha's pure body. Each ray is made up of countless miniature Buddhas going out to help all beings and then dissolving back into Buddha's body when their work is done.

2 Feel the power of the Buddha, recalling his abilities and willingness to help you. Practicing Buddhists would take refuge in the Buddha, by repeating with conviction three times: "I take refuge in the Buddha, the Dharma (teachings) and the Sangha (spiritual community of Buddhist custodians of the teachings)."

3 Make a request from your heart to become free from negativity, misunderstandings and all other

impediments to receiving enlightenment. Feel that your request is accepted and a stream of purifying white light flows from the Buddha's heart and enters you through the top of your head, instantly eradicating the darkness that is your negative energy. Simultaneously recite Shakyamuni's mantra, feeling the white light continuously drawing the mantra's enlightening energy from the Buddha's heart directly into your own heart.

4 Continue this mantra and visualization until your body feels light and imbued with bliss. Then dwell on this feeling for a while.

5 If you have managed the above visualization and are ready for more, visualize a golden light descending from Buddha's heart into your body via the crown of your head, as you recite the mantra. The golden light represents Buddha's wisdom, giving you strength and inspiration, whereas the white light represents purification of negative attributes.

6 Finally, if you can keep your focus just a little longer, visualize yourself surrounded by all the living beings who fill the vastness of space. As you recite the mantra, radiate love and compassion for them, carried on rays of light emanating from your heart. Contemplate the wisdom that they all want to achieve freedom from suffering and happiness, just as you do. You might even imagine them all transforming into Buddhas, experiencing great wisdom and bliss.

OM MANI PADME HUM (AUM MANAY PADMAY HUM. HUM can alternatively be pronounced HUNG)
The mantra of Avalokiteshvara – 'compassion'

Avalokiteshvara, which means "He who looks with an unwavering eye," is the embodiment of the infinite compassion of all the Buddhas. In Tibet, he is known as Chenrezig. Avalokiteshvara's gaze is able to look upon all beings in all realms as he wishes for their liberation from suffering.

Buddhism holds that a person can be reborn into any of six realms, according to karmic causes and effects, either literally or allegorically. For example, if your actions caused the starvation of others, particularly as a result of your greed, some day karma would cause you to be in a situation of insatiable hunger, not as a retribution or permanent imprisonment, but as a natural rebalancing process. According to tradition, this could manifest itself as a literal rebirth into a realm called the 'hungry ghost realm,' where you have the desire to eat

but cannot. This may actually refer to the state of one's consciousness suffering in limbo after death and before being reborn, or it could mean that, as a living human, you inherit circumstances of great hunger that cannot be appeased.

Each syllable of Avalokiteshvara's mantra is directed to one of the six realms. One practice is to visualize with the mantra an appropriately colored light permeating all beings in each realm (see the table on page 126). You then radiate white or golden light towards them to supplant the color of the realm they are in, for the purpose of alleviating their suffering and helping to lead them towards enlightenment. If you subscribe to the idea of literal realms, you can visualize your light radiating to images of gods and demigods, as depicted in Buddhist art. For that, you need to source the relevant images to get accurate representations of these beings.

An easier practice is to consider that, within our human realm, the other five realms exist as metaphors. In this way we can observe that some people seem to have everything and are happy, so for a while they are in an allegorical 'god' realm. They consequently lose touch with the real world and, because of complacency, fail to develop spiritual attributes and eventually suffer from lack of fulfillment at a deep level. Other people are like 'demigods,' who seem to have a lot of power, but are beset by jealousy of others with more power. Some people are living as 'fortunate' humans whose circumstances allow them the time and inclination to see that compassion and wisdom are worthwhile attributes, and are open to developing those qualities. Such people are considered to have had a 'precious rebirth,' as compared to other less fortunate humans whose circumstances cause them to live as if they were in another realm less conducive to spiritual practice. Some people are living like animals, lacking the intelligence to prevent themselves being exploited by others. Then there is the hungry ghost state, as described earlier. Finally, there are those who continuously suffer horribly with painful disease and misfortune, and are experiencing life as hell on earth.

Use the table on the following page to match the color of the realm with the beings in it. Those colors basically represent the negative state that those beings are in. Then visualize white or golden light emanating from you to them, which washes away the negative color relating to the suffering of that realm.

If you find the visualization too difficult, just repeat the mantra. It will still eventually evoke an increased level of compassion within you, purely through the power of the sound. With visualization or not, this mantra is designed to counter the negative forces that lock us into the miseries of existence within the six realms.

Syllable	Realm	Color
OM	gods	white
MA	demigods	green
NI	humans	yellow
PAD	animals	blue
ME	hungry ghosts	red
HUM	hell-beings	black

Note: It is not suggested that any of these colors are inherently or objectively bad. It simply means that each color evokes both a positive and negative influence. So, the 'gods' in the god realm, or the humans living like gods in the human realm, will have their complacency reduced if the white light of their realm is replaced by a golden light. On the other hand, hell-beings, or humans living like they are in hell, could do with a bit of god-like comfort to counteract their suffering. Hence, driving out the black color with a white light would help achieve that. Colors conform to the laws of balance, or 'yin-yang,' one of which states that when something reaches its extreme, it changes into its opposite. For example, if you are extremely active, you will get exhausted and be forced to take rest.

White symbolizes purity, triumph and innocence, which are useful qualities to have, but if there was nothing but white, it would engender a pure sterility, a triumphant complacency, and an innocent naivety and blindness. This would add up to a state seemingly free of suffering, but which stifles further personal development.

Green symbolizes balance, contentment and harmony, as epitomized by the greenery of nature on a relaxing day. However, prolonged exposure to green with the exclusion of all other colors would turn that contentment into a mode of anger and jealousy, as expressed in the term 'green with envy.'

Yellow symbolizes the light of the sun and the enlightenment of human awareness. An excess of yellow would give a tremendous sense of self-awareness, but if it could be substituted for its closely related color gold, the gold would transmute that self-awareness to a more universal awareness.

Blue is the color of expansiveness, like the clear blue sky or the ocean, and signifies depth of thought and wisdom. On the other hand, if exposure to blue excludes other colors over a prolonged period, it will engender fear and ignorance, the hallmark of the animal realm.

Red is a very passionate color, which activates and warms. Many cold and impersonal people could do with a little of this warming color. However, red without any other color would cause an excessive desire to consume, like flames that consume everything they touch. Wanting to consume more than you can actually reach is the bane of the hungry ghost realm.

Black can have an alluring mystical beauty and excite a sense of mystery. But prolonged and total blackness indicates a complete absence of light. It therefore represents the unknown, and it is from the unknown that fear is born. A completely black environment would engender a state of utter despair. Hell, whether allegorical or literal, is represented by black, often superimposed by the consuming flames of red. Visualize white light here, to balance the darkness.

OM WAGI SHARE MUM
The mantra of Manjushri – 'wisdom'

Manjushri is the embodiment of all the wisdom of all the Buddhas. Golden light symbolizes wisdom, and ultimately helps generate it. Hence, Manjushri is himself golden-orange in color. In his right hand he holds the flaming double-edged sword of wisdom (as a metaphor for cutting through ignorance). In his left hand he holds the stem of a lotus attached to a lotus flower that is supporting a volume of the *Perfection of Wisdom Sutras*. Repeating the mantra of Manjushri along with visualizing his image is an excellent practice to develop wisdom, or as a complement to the contemplation of the essence of wisdom.

OM BADZA PANI HUNG
The mantra of Vajrapani – 'invincible power over negativity'

Whereas compassion is personified in Avalokiteshvara, and wisdom by Manjushri, Vajrapani represents the power and means to put our compassion and wisdom into effect. He is depicted as a wrathful entity, partly to underpin the fact that he represents raw power,

which, if used wisely, skillfully and with guidance, can lead to enlightenment in one lifetime. If used without guidance and skill, such power can be very injurious. Shakyamuni Buddha is said to have entrusted Vajrapani with the powerful esoteric teachings known as the Tantras. Thus, he is sometimes referred to as 'Lord of the Secret'.

Unlike most other meditational deities, Vajrapani is shown in an active, standing position rather than a passive seated posture. This gives further impact to the image of power and action that he is meant to portray. Vajrapani is, however, sometimes depicted in peaceful form, which illustrates that skillful use of compassion, wisdom, and power can be made in many diverse ways. In his right hand, Vajrapani wields a diamond-hard sceptre, called a vajra, as a symbol of the power of full spiritual awakening, and which lends him his name.

The full power of Vajrapani can only be tapped through initiation into the tantric methods of the Vajrayana path (which means 'thunderbolt' or 'lightning-quick' method). Initiation is something that very few people receive, and only if they are deemed able to deal with such precarious and powerful energies, and possess correct motivation. However, the ordinary person can simply recite this mantra without initiation into tantra, and still gain tremendous energy from it to propel their spiritual quest.

OM TARE TUTTARE TURE SOHA
The mantra of Green Tara (The Swift Liberator) – 'helpfulness over obstacles'

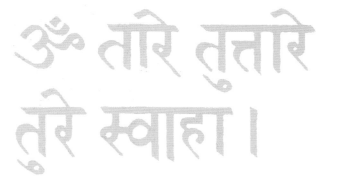

In Buddhism, Tara is the primary female expression of enlightenment, and affectionately considered the mother of Buddhas past, present and future. She is referred to as the 'Swift Liberator' because she has the attributes of a nurturing mother goddess who rapidly rushes to one's aid when called upon. There are many accounts in many cultures of a mother deity figure who appears in times of need in response to prayer or invocation. Interestingly then, stories of the manifestations of the Virgin Mary and those of Tara are essentially similar.

Tara is often invoked to answer seemingly mundane prayers, but her true power lies in the ability to guide one towards swift liberation. She is particularly adept at helping the seeker to overcome eight internal fears: pride, hindrance, anger, envy, wrong views, avarice, attachment and doubt.

Tara appears in many forms. As Green Tara, she represents compassion in action. This is because green is symbolic of the wind element, which has the quality of rapid movement.

OM TARE TUTTARE TURE MAMA ARYU PUNI GYANYA PUNDING GURUYE SOHA
The mantra of White Tara – 'long life mantra'

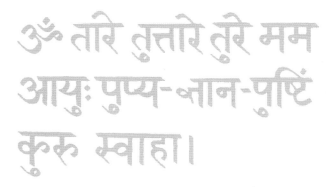

Tara emanating as White Tara is associated with practices specifically aimed at increasing life span and overcoming obstacles that might hinder a long life.

She can be invoked to help deal with your own hindrances or those of another person, in which case the meditator will imagine himself or herself to be Tara, recite the White Tara mantra, and hold the image of the afflicted person in his or her heart, bathed in a purifying white light.

Invoking Tara for overcoming severe, life-threatening illnesses is a very common practice amongst Tibetans. Often a Tibetan doctor will supplement whatever treatment he is prescribing with recommending a one-day Tara puja. This involves constant repetition of the White Tara mantra along with the commissioning of a painting of White Tara that must be completed within 24 hours. This intense focus on Tara and her attributes often has the desired effect because, like everything else, disease is the manifestation of a vibration, and all vibrations can be altered.

Mantras from other religions

It is not the intention of this book to give a comprehensive and exhaustive interpretation of all mantras from all cultures. The examples just given represent just a few from a huge range of mantras. Here are a few classic mantras from the Mayan, Islamic, and Christian traditions. Chant them as an exercise to see where their syllables resonate in your body.

Mantra	Tradition of origin
K'IN (K-EEN)	Mayan
WOE YA	Native American
ALLAH HU	Islamic/Sufi
ALLELUIA (AHL-LAY-LOO-YAH)	Christian

AIDS FOR THE PRACTICE OF JAPA

Keeping track of how many times you have recited your mantra is important because you will usually be aiming to fulfill a specific number of repetitions. The most common tool for this purpose is a string of beads. Islam, Christianity, Judaism, and all the eastern religions and spiritual practices have their versions of this. Catholic Christians, for example, use rosary beads; the eastern practices use mala beads. In both cases the principle is the same: you check off a given number of beads with your thumb until the required number of mantras has been completed. The physical act of rhythmically thumbing the beads has the added bonus of helping to maintain your focus on the practice.

Mantras are usually recommended to be repeated at least 21 times, but 108 are considered the effective minimum for dedicated practice. A japa mala therefore consists of 108 beads. Because the japa mala is a continuous circle of beads, there is an additional bead called a meru, which is slightly larger and acts as a reference point to indicate when one mala of repetitions (108 repetitions) has been completed. When the meru is reached, the beads are reversed in the hand

and one continues counting the beads in the opposite direction. Japa is therefore conducted in multiples of 108 mantra repetitions. A particularly extensive japa session with a deity mantra is known as a purascharana, which involves the repetition of the mantra 100,000 times for each of its syllables. Therefore, an extensive mantra such as the Maha Mantra that has 32 syllables, or the Maha Mrityunjaya that has 34 syllables, would take several years to complete.

The thumb and third finger roll the beads. The index finger is not used, because to do so is traditionally considered to have a negative effect upon the process. This is because the index finger is associated with activities such as picking your nose, cleaning your ears and so on. In many traditions, the mala beads should not hang below the navel. Also, when not in use, they should be wrapped and stored in a clean cloth.

Japa meditation using deity mantras usually begins by invoking the aid of the relevant deity. Often there is also a concluding ritual. For example, a Buddhist might offer the benefits gained to the welfare and future enlightenment of all beings. If you are extensively practicing deity japa, you will have received initiation into the procedure by a qualified teacher or guru. That teacher will have taught you the necessary invocations and rituals for that tradition.

You can recite the mantras aloud (vaikhari japa), as a whisper (upamsu japa) or mentally (manasika japa). Mental japa is considered the most powerful, but also the most difficult because it requires greater mental focus. Reciting aloud has the advantage of the voice acting as a solid anchor for the attention, but restricts the places where you can practice without drawing unsympathetic attention to yourself. Mental japa of course has the advantage of allowing you to repeat mantras even while you are doing routine manual activities. Most practitioners use all of these methods in varying proportions, just for variety, because it is easy to become drowsy, or even doze off.

As an adjunct to mental and audible japa, one can repeatedly write the mantra into a notebook reserved for this purpose, ideally with a pen reserved for the same purpose. It is not important which language is used for the written mantras (known as likhita japa), because it is the sound vibration evoked in your mind that holds the power. The most important thing is to ensure that the mantra, whether repeated physically or mentally, has the correct phonetic pronunciation.

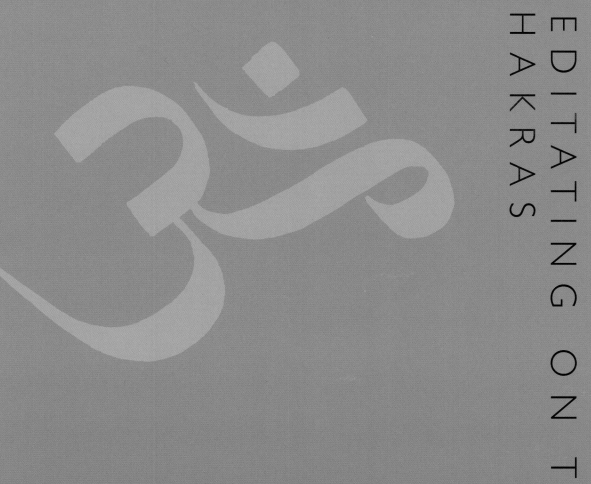

MEDITATING ON THE
CHAKRAS

Many people who read this type of book have heard about chakras, and know that they are vortices of energy located at intervals between the base of the spine and the crown of the head. It is very common to hear people talk about them in relation to healing, auras and personal growth, and quite often you can come across people who advocate meditating upon them, to 'open' them. Perhaps less well known is the fact that, if you are not fully informed about these energies or you are insufficiently prepared in body and mind, you risk doing more harm than good.

'Chakra' is the Sanskrit word for 'wheel'. One clear and widely accepted definition of chakras is: 'focal points along the central channel upon which one's concentration is directed during the completion stage of highest yoga tantra'. Since very few full-time meditators are selected to enter even the beginning stage of lowest yoga tantra, this definition underscores the importance of being careful with these practices. Consequently, an explanation of chakras and their associated energies is very useful, so that we can avoid the risks and benefit from the safe practices.

NADIS

Yogic theory states that there are 72,000 nadis within the energy field of the body. Nadi literally translates as 'tube' or 'tubular organ', and in this context means 'tubular organ of the subtle body through which energy flows.' Nadis are described as having three concentric layers, one inside the other, similar to the insulation of an electric wire. These layers are also similar to those of a nerve fibre and of a blood vessel as seen in cross-section. Some authorities believe the nadis include the blood vessels and nerves as well as the invisible channels for prana (energy) distribution. Others include the nerves but not the blood vessels, while others consider them to exclude nerves and blood vessels, existing purely as energetic or 'psychic' channels within the energy body, which westerners might call the astral body.

The most important nadi is the sushumna, which corresponds to the position of the spinal cord, and along which the chakras are located. Either side of the sushumna we have the ida and pingala nadis. The ida represents the sedating energy of the moon and influences the parasympathetic nervous system (the resting responses). This nadi begins at the left nostril and is activated by the breath entering that nostril. The pingala represents the activating energy of the sun and influences the sympathetic nervous system (the awakening responses). This nadi begins at the right nostril and is activated by breath entering that nostril.

While there is breath there is life. So as you breathe, energy descends down the ida and pingala nadis to the base of the spine, where it connects with a dormant energy known as kundalini. As the ida and pingala energies descend, they intersect each other through the sushumna at various intervals, thus creating the vortices of energy known as chakras. These chakras are fundamental forces that regulate the functioning of the body/mind, and each represents a different state of consciousness.

As stated earlier, there are 72,000 nadis in total, and these will in fact include all the meridians and their branches as described in Chinese medicine. Probably there aren't exactly 72,000 nadis, because in classical texts on Indian philosophies, 144,000 is said to be the approximate length of a world cycle or 'age', but also seems to be a numerical statement which means a 'phenomenal amount'. Thus, 72,000, which is half of a 'phenomenal amount', seems to be another way of saying 'rather a lot'.

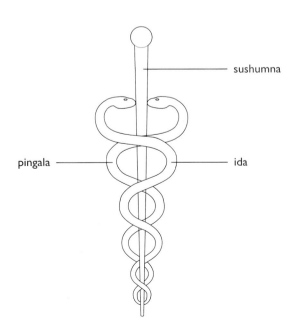

pingala — — ida

sushumna

THE KUNDALINI SHAKTI

The word 'kundalini' means a 'coiled female serpent'. Hence, it is a metaphoric description of the cosmic energy that is symbolized as a sleeping coiled serpent lying dormant at the base of the spinal column, within the muladhara (or root) chakra. For the aspirant to achieve full enlightenment, this latent power has to be aroused and encouraged to ascend the sushumna nadi, piercing each chakra on the way until the sahasrara chakra at the crown of the head is pierced and activated. Kundalini yoga or tantric yoga is a way of making this happen rapidly. However, no matter how you reach enlightenment or how long it takes, by definition enlightenment will coincide with the sahasrara chakra becoming fully 'opened'.

To accelerate the rising of the kundalini safely, control of the breath (pranayama) must be mastered, through the application of various bodily locks, or muscular contractions (called bandhas) and seals (called mudras). Usually, the posture first has to be realigned through the practice of hatha yoga asanas (postures). The kundalini is then coaxed upwards through specific meditations upon the chakras.

Yogic theory uses the metaphor of Siva to represent the latent illuminating power resident within the sahasrara (crown) chakra. Also, because the kundalini is a microcosm of the cosmic substrata, it is called kundalini shakti. The metaphor thus extends to enlightenment being a union between shakti (the female energy principle) and Lord Siva.

The Daoists of ancient China developed similar practices, albeit with different terminology. They named the practices 'internal elixir' methods (nei dan). Aspects of these Daoist methods are described later in this book, within the context of meditations for health and longevity.

The kundalini is closely related to sexual energy, so sexual abstinence is practiced, along with methods to transform aroused sexual energy into a 'propulsion fuel' to motivate the kundalini's ascent through the sushumna. Many westerners have latched onto this idea of transforming aroused sexual energy and seem to believe that this is the main point of tantra. Therefore, some people claim to practice tantric sex, which often seems to be an excuse for having more sex with a pseudospiritual endorsement attached. 'Tantra' is the Sanskrit word for 'thread' or 'continuity', implying a method carefully passed on and practiced under narrowly strict guidelines and continuous supervision. As a result of this implication of strict continuity, tantra is the name given to the advanced Buddhist texts and discourses that present

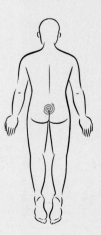

precise methods for achieving full enlightenment quickly. Tantra involves strict initiation into the practice of invocation and devotion towards a particular meditational deity. These teachings are not given lightly, so, even amongst ordained Buddhist monks, only a small percentage are given the practices based on tantra, and they do not spend their time having sex! Sexual transmutation within the sexual act is far more commonly practiced within the equivalent Daoist tantric systems, albeit by a minority of initiates as a small part of a wider practice.

The sushumna nadi

The sushumna nadi is said to be fiery-red by those who have 'connected' with it through meditation. It begins from the muladhara chakra, at the second coccygeal vertebra (base of the spine). From there it rises through the entire vertebral canal and reaches an aperture at the crown of the head known to yogis as the brahma-randhra. This aperture is where the consciousness is said to leave the body at death. In babies this aperture is a soft space between the cranial bones and is known anatomically as the anterior fontanelle.

The sushumna has several subdivisions within it. Inside the sushumna is the vajra nadi, which is said to be as brilliant as a diamond in the sun. The vajra nadi contains the pale-colored chitra nadi, which is considered the most important energy pathway in the body. Hence it is referred to as the 'heavenly way'. At the beginning of the chitra nadi, and within it, is a natural obstruction to the kundalini called the brahma granthi, which means 'knot of brahma'. This obstruction must first be penetrated before the kundalini can rise up to the head.

Within the chitra nadi is a minute nadi called the Brahma nadi, which runs through the central canal of the spinal cord. It is specifically through the Brahma nadi that the kundalini flows.

All the main chakras exist within the minute brahma nadi. Most people think of the chakras as being fairly large energetic 'wheels' that present themselves as spinning in a vertical plane, much like you would view the wheel of a car. In fact they are minute vortices that are actually experienced as spinning in a horizontal plane. In other words, you would see their circularity if you could look through the brahma nadi as if it were a telescope, but you would only see them edge on by looking at the body from the front.

Although the chakras themselves are minute, their direct reverberating influence extends to the corresponding nerve plexuses in the physical body. They have been described as storehouses for the vital energy, and aspects of consciousness, awareness, and bliss.

If a chakra is chosen as a focus for meditation, it is visualized as a lotus with a specific number of petals. The petals are actually specific nadis emanating from the chakra, giving the appearance of a lotus. These nadis or 'petals' hang slightly downwards when the kundalini is dormant, and turn slightly upwards when the kundalini ascends and activates that chakra, just as rising sap would animate the petals of a drooping flower.

Each nadi that emanates from a given chakra vibrates as the kundalini passes through that chakra, producing a latent sound conforming to one of the fifty Sanskrit syllables. In other words, each petal is associated with a Sanskrit syllable. When meditating upon a chakra to the extent whereby the kundalini begins to flow through it, these vibrations can be felt.

The number of nadis or petals emanating from each chakra is given in the following table. This table gives the name and location of each main chakra, along with some other key associations.

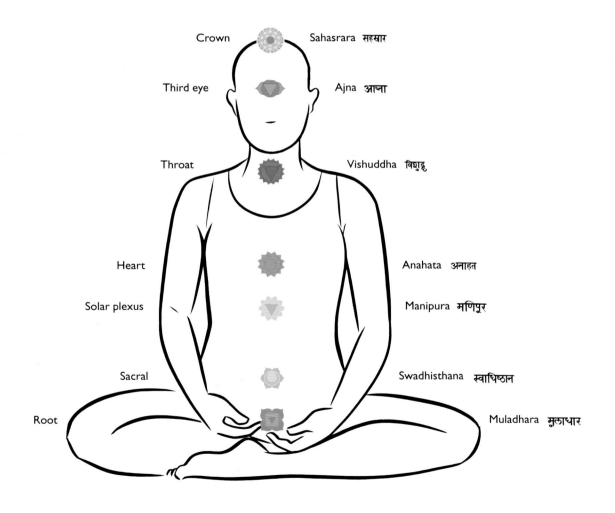

Table of chakra correspondences

Chakra and its position	Related nerve plexus	Element	Gland	Sense	Physical structure and functions governed	Effects arising from extensive meditation on this chakra	Bija (seed) mantra	Number of ema-nating nadis or 'petals'	Presiding deity
Muladhara Coccyx	Sacral	Earth	Adrenals	Smell	Kidneys Spinal column	Direct awareness of kundalini; control of breath and mind.	Lam	4	Brahma
Swadhis-thana Genitals	Prostatic	Water	Gonads	Taste	Reproductive system	Intuition; awareness of entities in other realms; many impure qualities are purged.	Vam	6	Vishnu
Manipura Navel	Solar	Fire	Pancreas	Sight	Stomach Liver Gall bladder Nervous system	All disease and fear of fire is eliminated; will power.	Ram	10	Rudra
Anahata Heart	Cardiac	Air	Thymus	Touch	Heart Circulatory system	Psychic powers; compassion.	Yam	12	Isha
Vishuddha Throat	Laryngeal	Ether	Thyroid	Hearing	Bronchial tubes Vocal cords Lungs	Enhanced communication skills.	Ham	16	Sadasiva
Ajna Between eyes	Cavernous		Pituitary		Lower brain Left eye	Clarity of thought; insight.	OM	2	Paramasiva
Sahasrara Top of head			Pineal		Upper brain Right eye	Higher consciousness.	Beyond sound	1000	Siva

Crown	Sahasrana	सहस्रार
Third eye	Ajna	आज्ञा
Throat	Vishuddha	विशुद्ध
Heart	Anahata	अनाहत
Solar plexus	Manipura	मणिपूर
Sacral	Swadhisthana	स्वाधिष्ठान
Root	Muladhara	मूलाधार

Each chakra also has a particular color and geometric form, as illustrated in the diagrams of the chakras.

When meditating upon the chakras, you can either focus your mind upon the relevant location within the spinal cord, or you can focus more on the front of your body, using the locations listed in the first column of the table of chakra correspondences. Either way, concentration should start at the lowest chakra (muladhara) and progress to the highest (sahasrara). An erect and vertical spine is essential to give a direct and open conduit within which the kundalini can rise. The kundalini literally rises upwards, away from the earth's surface. Therefore, if you are lying down or bent over, so that the sushumna is not aligned vertically, the movement of the kundalini will be impeded. This is why great emphasis is placed on preparing the body so that you can sit comfortably erect for extended periods of time.

A good method for focusing upon the chakras is to fix your attention on the lowest chakra and chant OM either aloud or internally, varying the pitch until you feel the sound 'connect' with that location. Then move to the next chakra, raising the pitch of OM until a connection is made. You will find that the higher the chakra, the higher the pitch. To begin with, try chanting OM at random pitches and feel where the sound connects in your body. You will find the effect is very clear, especially at the heart and throat chakras.

Getting the kundalini to awaken from its slumber and rise upwards through the chakras is not easy. It requires extensive preparation and purification practices over many months. Also, as said before, and stressed again, it must be done under the close supervision of one who has mastered the process. Once the kundalini is awakened, it must be coaxed upwards from one chakra to the next. Invariably it will descend back down, so the process will be a two steps forward, one step back affair, with the occasional three steps back. How quickly the kundalini can be raised and how long it can be kept at a particular chakra depends upon the purity, self-discipline, motivation and evolution of the meditator. It will not get to the sahasrara chakra unless the desire for liberation is as much of a thirst for water is to one who is dehydrating in the desert. Such desire for illumination comes only to those who are pure of heart and have evolved beyond the need to indulge the ego. In other words, one must be considerably evolved already to get the kundalini to make the full journey and stay at the sahasrara.

Can we imagine what it is like to have the kundalini fully awakened? Those who have reached that state describe it as ultimate knowledge, freedom, love, connectedness and bliss. In comparison, our lives often seem very unsatisfactory and mundane.

What then, is the point of us lesser mortals even knowing about these theories? Firstly, they are very interesting. Secondly, if you are genuinely interested, it probably means that a significant level of spiritual evolution has occurred within you. After all, there are many other 'lesser' subjects you could be reading about compared to a book on meditation. Who knows? Perhaps you are ready to raise your kundalini all the way (only with a proper guide, remember). Thirdly, you can lower your realistic expectations and not expect to get your kundalini to blossom into the sahasrara chakra during this lifetime. Instead, know that the chakras are excellent subjects or objects for the purpose of finding out about yourself and for rebalancing your emotions, thoughts and physical functions.

QI AND THE DAO

Meditation is really about keeping your consciousness mindfully relating to the present. Most of this book so far has been about that. As a positive side effect, general improvements in health and increasing your chances of a longer life can be a useful by-product of meditation, mainly because meditation helps you to accept and cope with stress more effectively. However, meditations exist which are designed specifically for the maximizing of good health and longevity, either as ends in themselves or based on the idea that the longer you live, the wiser you should become, thus increasing your chances of reaching enlightenment in this lifetime. The philosophy that has developed these practices most thoroughly is Daoism.

Daoist meditation is the method developed by the ancient Chinese, the roots of which date back about 7,000 years. The word 'Dao' literally means 'the way', and by implication means the 'natural way'. It is based on a detailed observation of nature and its cycles, and of how we, as humans, naturally reflect nature and harmonize with it. It recognizes certain laws and principles of nature that, if adhered to, lead to good health and longevity. Conversely, living one's life in opposition to these fundamental laws inevitably leads to problems that will compromise health and longevity.

Good health and longevity constitute the main preoccupation in Daoist practices and, because of this, the traditional healing arts of China were formulated by Daoist exponents. These included methods to extend one's own life and vitality, which we now call internal qigong, from which Daoist meditation is derived. It also included methods to heal and prevent illness in others, which includes all branches of traditional oriental medicine, including herbalism, acupuncture, various bodywork therapies and ways of transmitting qi via healing qigong. The oldest detailed resource on oriental medicine, the *Huang Ti Nei Jing Su Wen*, was believed to have been written in around 2550 BCE by the legendary Yellow Emperor Huang Ti.

Buddhism was imported into China in around 58 CE, and not long after, a Daoist by the name of Zhang Dao-Ling combined the traditional Daoist meditation practices with Buddhism and created a religion called Dao Jiao. Later on, Tibetan Buddhists were invited to China to share some of their practices for the enrichment of meditation in China. Thus, Daoist meditation today is essentially traditional Daoist, influenced by some Tibetan Buddhist attributes.

Daoist meditation and most Tibetan Buddhist meditation are characterized by proactive use of the mind, meaning that the power of visualization and imagery is strongly developed. Visualization in Daoist meditation means detecting and leading subtle energies along specific pathways in the body, ultimately to 'open' the mind as well as transform potential or actual sickness into health.

To appreciate Daoist meditation fully, it is first necessary to understand certain Daoist concepts such as qi and yin-yang.

Qi as a broad concept is the substrata of the entire universe. It includes everything in the universe from the most material to the immaterial. Therefore, within its broadest possible definition, we can consider a rock as qi and we can think of an individual as qi. However, in practice, qi is generally thought of as the invisible factors that bind matter together and activate all things, including the things that are tangible but invisible to our senses. Visible and palpable things, such as rocks, are collectively known as xing, whereas amorphous, invisible phenomena such as wind, smell, heat, movement or even happiness all fall under the general heading of qi. Therefore to exist physically requires qi, to move and feel requires qi and to think requires qi.

You could say that xing is all those things you can perceive and count, whereas qi is all that which you cannot see or count. Another angle on this way of perceiving the universe is to consider that initially, things in the xing category seem permanent, but the fact that all things are impermanent shows that they are constantly subject to change, however imperceptible that change may seem. The agents of change are those invisible factors called qi.

Traditional Daoist philosophy considers the universe to be driven by three manifestations of qi: heaven qi (tian qi), earth qi (di qi) and human qi (ren qi). Heaven qi is the largest and most powerful of these forces, because it contains earth qi within it (the earth itself being a planet within the heavens). Earth qi is regarded as the earth's magnetic field combined with the earth's underground heat, which is believed to produce a matrix of energy lines and zones across and through the planet. Earthquakes and volcanic activity are thus seen as the earth qi rebalancing itself.

From our point of view, as beings standing upon this planet, heaven qi is considered to be the combined forces from above that exert influence upon the earth. These include energy, gravity and light from the sun, moon and stars, the forces that in turn govern the climate. The climate, like everything else, is subject to fluctuation, so extremes of weather, including tornadoes and torrential rain, are seen as heaven qi trying to restore balance.

The interaction of heaven qi with earth qi can be observed in other examples, such as too much heat from the sun and too little rain causing crops on the earth to fail in a drought. It can therefore be said that earth qi absorbs heaven qi and is influenced by it.

Human qi (and also animal qi) is seen as a melding of the forces of heaven qi and earth qi. Human qi is a type of energy field which draws heaven qi downwards from above and earth qi upwards from below. The balance of our human qi is therefore strongly influenced by the natural cycles of heaven qi and earth qi.

Harmonizing ourselves with the forces and cycles of heaven and earth is the core philosophy of Daoism (the study and practice of how to follow the harmonious laws of nature), from which Daoist meditation and qigong developed. Daoists have observed that nature constantly repeats itself, so if you carefully observe nature, you can gain insight into the way nature cyclically rebalances its qi.

Daoist qigong meditation (hereafter referred to as 'longevity meditation') therefore directly aims to influence our human qi, which permeates and animates our body and mind, by way of harmonizing the entry and exit of both heaven qi and earth qi, and by regulating the flow of qi within us.

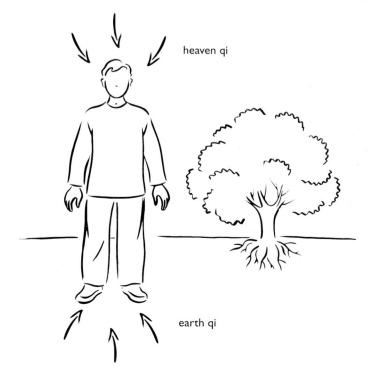

heaven qi

earth qi

In terms of our health, we can consider qi to be that factor which animates us into life. Therefore, our vitality and 'aliveness' is a reflection of our level and adequate distribution of qi. If we lack qi, or if its flow is impeded in some way, then we will lack vitality and may become ill. Within this more narrow definition of qi, we can equate it to our 'life force'. Thus we can simply say that the difference between that which is alive and that which is not alive is the presence or absence of 'aliveness', called 'qi' or 'chi' in Chinese and 'ki' in Japanese. It also roughly equates to prana in the Indian yogic systems.

Western traditions view our life force as an esoteric phenomenon, generally accepted by us as a gift from greater powers. As such, westerners have not tried to understand it to the extent their oriental counterparts have. The oriental traditions see our 'aliveness' and therefore our energy and vitality as much more to do with our interaction with nature's cycles. Daoist philosophy is basically a way of describing and understanding how we harmonize with our environment. It is to do with understanding how all things are ultimately striving to maintain a level of interdependence.

While we are alive, qi or 'aliveness' permeates every part of our body, keeping each cell and every bodily function alive. Although cells are dying throughout our body, they are constantly being replaced. The replacement of cells declines as we get older until not enough of the essential ones necessary for correct organic functioning are replaced. At that time we malfunction and die. The more qi that reaches the cells, the less prone to decay they will be, so that an abundant supply of qi to a cell means a healthier cell. However, it is not simply a question of quantity, but also of movement. All living things exhibit more activity than their dead counterparts. Qi flows smoothly and abundantly in a cycle within healthy, vibrant creatures. Unhealthy creatures are not vibrant, because their qi is not flowing smoothly.

It may be that qi is not present in an adequate quantity to generate sufficient momentum for a smooth flow, resulting in some areas being starved of vitality while other areas stagnate and accumulate waste products, rather like insufficient water failing to flush debris from a drainage pipe. Alternatively, it may be that too much qi is accumulating in a particular area of the body, causing stagnation or hyperactivity there. This is rather like too many cars on a constricted road, resulting in no cars moving and causing potential or actual irritation and aggression (such as road rage in traffic jams). So, to remain healthy or to regain health, qi must be restored if it is deficient, unblocked if it is stuck, or calmed if it is irritated. One way or another it must be kept moving.

Such imbalances in the quantity and circulation of qi have many causes, which include emotional disturbance, shock, unbalanced mental attitude, excessive heat or cold, extreme assault from virulent organisms, poisons, poor diet, incorrect use of the body (creating postural/organ stress) and accidents.

We have established that we must have qi to live and more qi to move. However, living involves a process of organic change ranging from birth and growth towards eventual decay. The underlying factor enabling birth, growth and reproduction is known as jing (pronounced 'ching') which translates as 'essence'. Jing determines your constitutional strength and is the blueprint for your individual characteristics. In western physiological terms it roughly equates to your hormonal system insofar as it is your hormones that regulate growth, reproduction, decay and other changes in your body.

However, an organism can exist with sufficient jing to fulfil the involuntary process of growth and reproduction without exhibiting an indication of consciousness. Consciousness signifies the presence of shen, which is the energy behind the power to think and discriminate, to rationalize and to reflect on the self. Without shen there can be no personality. Qi, jing and shen are known in traditional oriental thinking as the 'three treasures'. So in summary, we can say that everything has some degree of qi. Only that which is living in the sense that it is subject to

THE THREE TREASURES

growth, reproduction and decay has jing. Only creatures that are conscious and can reflect on the self (humans) have shen (although this is the traditional Daoist view – it could be that other animals do have shen. We do not really know). It is important to remember though, that jing and shen are limited aspects or special manifestations of qi, as is everything else that exists. They are not really isolated in separate 'boxes' and, in practice, the borders between them can overlap.

How this information relates to your practice of meditation for good health and long life is that the main goal of all Daoist training is to learn how to retain your jing (constitutional strength), strengthen and regulate your qi flow and illuminate your shen (consciousness).

More about jing (essence)

Jing is a sort of concentrated qi awaiting mobilization. There are two forms of jing or 'essence': that acquired before birth and that acquired after birth. Jing acquired before birth is passed onto you during conception as a union between the jing stored in the sperm of your father and jing stored in the ovum of your mother. In the Chinese language, sperm is called 'jing zi', which means 'essence of the son', because it contains the jing passed from father to child. So we can see the parallel between genetics and jing. After conception, while the foetus is still in the womb, it continues to receive jing from the mother through the umbilical cord. It therefore follows that if your parents were healthy at the time of your conception, and your mother lived a healthy lifestyle throughout your time in her womb, then your 'prebirth essence' will be strong.

This essence acquired before birth is stored in the kidneys and is largely fixed in quantity and quality at birth, being slowly consumed during the normal process of living, until death from old age signifies its final depletion. However, overwork, poor diet and excessive sexual activity over a prolonged period will accelerate its depletion. On the other hand, its quality can be increased and its depletion significantly slowed down through the practice of Daoist longevity meditation (internal qigong), taiji quan (also known as t'ai ch'i ch'uan – a system of movement and awareness training) and certain types of yoga.

The term 'postbirth essence' is given to the jing that is extracted from food and refined by your digestive system once you have been born and thereafter throughout life. It supplements the prebirth essence, and together they form a generalized essence that underpins the functioning of your body/mind. This generalized essence is stored in your kidneys, and is therefore referred to as 'kidney essence'. Thus, jing is rather like a powerful battery, whereas qi is like electricity formed in that battery and which subsequently circulates to 'electrify' us into activity and growth.

The prebirth component of your jing is like an inheritance of cash invested for you to get you off to a good start in life. The postbirth component is like the interest earned from your investment plus the money you earn from day to day employment. If you withdraw your monetary investment and spend it, you will have no reserves and no more interest accruing. Therefore, you will have to work harder to maintain your comforts. Similarly, if you squander your prebirth essence, you will become progressively less robust in resisting ailments, and you will need to take much more care about how you live and what you eat. In other words, you will have to work harder to hold onto your health.

Jing, then, has various functions, all concerned with conception, growth, development and sexual maturation. It is said to fill 'the sea of marrow', which is a generic term for the bones, brain, spinal cord, all other nerve tissue and teeth. Your jing therefore determines your proper growth and development. In particular, it provides the basis for normal brain development.

Original qi

There are several types of qi that animate your body and mind, all basically the same but varying between more 'dense' and more 'rarefied' in quality, and labeled according to the specific job that qi does. The deepest, most fundamental manifestation of qi in your body is known as original qi, which is simply jing in a more dynamic phase.

Whereas jing mostly resides in the kidneys and circulates extremely slowly through the body, metaphorically like a viscous fluid, to provide the impetus for our physical growth, original qi is more energetic and flows everywhere.

The importance of jing and of original qi to Daoist meditation is the crux of the practice. Daoist longevity meditation aims to conserve and improve the quality of the jing stored in the kidneys, and by so doing improve the quantity and quality of original qi, so that all the organs and functions of the body can be imbued with life-enhancing vitality at a deep and sustained level. In a nutshell we can say that our level of original qi in circulation directly relates to our level of vitality, so having only a little means we will be constantly tired and having a lot means we will have more energy to get on with life.

The gate of vitality

Your ultimate source of internal warmth and bodily functions emanates from an area deep in your abdomen, more or less between your kidneys. This area is known as the gate of vitality (ming men) within which a heating factor known as 'life gate fire' transforms your jing into original qi. Within Daoist longevity meditation practice, the gate of vitality can be considered an aspect of your lower dantian. The lower dantian is an area in your lower abdomen that is like a vast sea of qi that ensures the filling of various reservoirs of qi within your body. One way of looking at the relationship between the gate of vitality and the lower dantian is to think of the lower dantian as a sea of jing which is acted upon by the life gate fire to cause some evaporation of that jing into a more active state called original qi, which then enlivens all the organs and functions of your body.

More about shen (mind)

Shen is usually translated as 'mind' or 'spirit'. It is your raw consciousness, in other words, the 'you' that looks out at the world and wonders at it. It basically refers to your higher consciousness, so it is that 'ingredient' which makes you human. Consequently, it can control other aspects of your mind, for example by giving you the ability to override your basic instincts instead of always succumbing to them. As a result, it gives the faculties of free will, consideration and contemplative thought. In a way, it is like a control tower that directs other facets of your mind, such as your will power, your ability to plan and decide, and your capacity to think.

In its role as a control tower, your shen has the power to direct your qi to fulfil your intent. The facet of your mind that enables you to think with clarity and intent is called yi. Therefore, when doing a meditation that involves focusing your attention

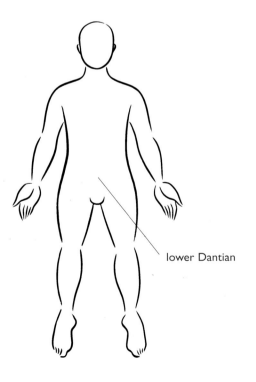

lower Dantian

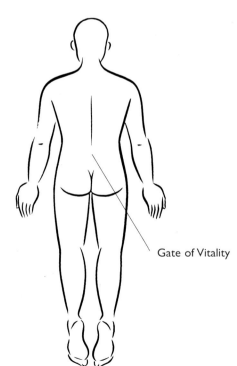

Gate of Vitality

clearly upon a function such as your breathing, or a concept such as compassion, the success with which you can maintain clarity of thought and mental focus is dependent on the strength of your yi (clear intent). Similarly, longevity meditations that involve you using your mind to influence a movement of qi somewhere in your body is an example of your yi leading your qi.

Since your yi is your conscious thought process, it requires a well-nourished and energized brain to manifest itself. The brain is nerve tissue, which in Daoist theory is an aspect of what they call 'marrow'. The proper development of the marrow, and therefore of the brain, depends on the quality and quantity of jing. Therefore, it is clear that the clarity of your mind also depends on the quality of your jing.

Jing, qi and shen, therefore, refer to three different levels of 'condensation' of qi. Jing is the most coarse and dense, qi is more rarefied than jing and shen is the most subtle and immaterial. In normal living, if your jing and qi are depleted, your shen will be dull.

The core concept of the three treasures can be summarized in the following table:

Jing (vital essence)	**Qi** (vital energy)	**Shen** (mind)
■ Determines substance	■ Enables function	■ Creates intention
■ Physical body	■ Energy body	■ Consciousness

We can now see from the above explanation of the three treasures that it is important to look after those treasures and utilize them for maximum benefit. After all, there is no point in allowing any type of treasure just to disappear, or to hoard it away and never benefit from it. The reasons for doing Daoist longevity meditations are listed here:

- ■ To help protect and maintain the quality of your jing, and thus extend the length and quality of your life.
- ■ To strengthen your kidneys, because they are where your jing is rooted and stored, and from where your original qi emanates after its conversion from jing (a process that takes place within the gate of vitality).
- ■ To keep your shen strong so that you can sustain concentration without distraction, and thus 'feel' and direct your qi.
- ■ To encourage a more efficient circulation of qi, which will, to a degree, result in a more efficient conversion of original qi from jing.
- ■ At a more advanced level, to control the generation of original qi from jing in a smooth, continuous stream.

To summarize the importance of the three treasures, we should remember that qi, jing and shen are interdependent. When your shen is weak, your qi will also be weak and lack force and direction, leading to accelerated degeneration of your body. Likewise, your qi energizes your shen and your jing ultimately nourishes it, so qi and jing keep your shen strong and sharp. Therefore if any of the three treasures are weak, the others will be weakened and your whole body/mind will pay the price.

To understand the essence of qigong further, you should know that qi is flowing everywhere throughout the living body, but aggregates into 'channels' of more concentrated qi flow. Here is an analogy: just as no part of your living body can be without qi, likewise no part of a sea can be without water. Some areas of the sea will have stronger currents, resulting from the dynamic movement and interaction of the sea and of the planet as a whole. Many of these currents can be charted (such as the Gulf Stream). Likewise, within a human or animal body, the general dynamic of being alive results in qi aggregating along discernible courses.

Over many millennia the Chinese have mapped out these channels (also called 'meridians'). They also noticed what happens when a channel does not flow in the way it should. As a result, they devised ways of restoring the correct 'attitude' of the channels and the qi within them. These 'ways' include all the methods of qigong, Daoist meditation and the oriental healing arts.

The channels or 'meridians' run like rivers all over

the surface of the body, continuing like subterranean streams deep into the interior of the body, directing qi into and away from all the internal organs. Where one channel begins and ends, it flows into another channel, so that you have a continuous circuit. Sometimes, a channel will also connect with other channels elsewhere along its course. From the main or primary channels, stream-like branches divide off at intervals, which themselves subdivide into more streams to supply qi to all the bodily structures, including muscles, fascia (connective tissue) and bone. The channel system is like a vast matrix supplying qi to all areas and functions of the body, allowing interaction throughout all aspects of the body and mind. This is similar to the ever-dividing and spreading profile of our nervous system and circulatory system. Specifically, we have 12 pairs of primary channels that, via surface and internal pathways, connect the extremities of our bodies to our internal organs, and by way of millions of tiny secondary offshoots, to all other areas of the body.

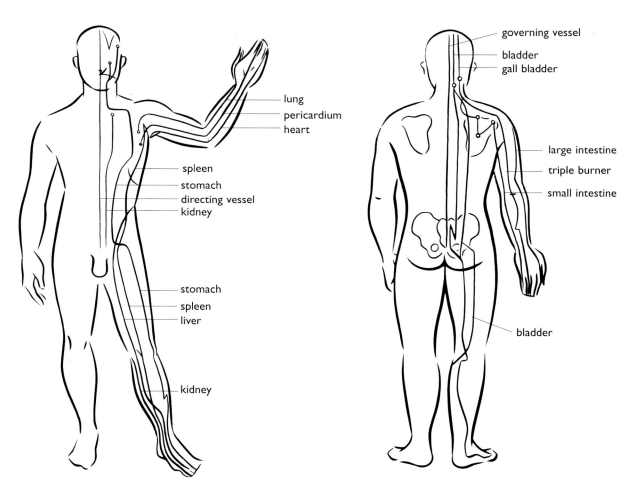

The primary channels of the body

In addition to the 12 primary channels, there are eight reservoirs of qi known as 'extraordinary vessels,' which top up the qi in the primary channels, or drain off excess qi from those channels, thus regulating the distribution and circulation of qi in your body. Two of these reservoirs have particular significance within the practice of qigong. These are the 'front mai', which runs down the vertical mid-line of your body on the front of your torso, and the 'back mai', which runs up the posterior mid-line of your body in two branches. One branch is called the 'fire path', which runs from your perineum via your coccyx up the posterior border of your spinal column, then over the mid-line of your cranium and down the front of your face into your palate to connect with the front mai, as the tongue touches the palate. The other branch, called the 'water path', diverges from the fire path at the base of the coccyx and runs through the marrow of your spinal cord, then through your brain, reconnecting with the fire path on the top of your head (see below). This path equates to the chitra nadi described earlier (see page 139).

Another important vessel or mai relevant to the Daoist meditator is the middle mai, which can be experienced and visualized as a vertical route of qi through the centre of your torso and head, just in front of your spine. Within advanced Daoist longevity meditation practice, the middle mai can actually be experienced as qi that moves vertically upwards from the lower dantian to just above the head, and moves downwards from the lower dantian to the perineum. Some practitioners experience it as a sky-blue light.

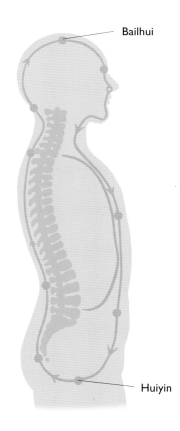

The fire path Qi circulation up the Back Mai and down the Front Mai

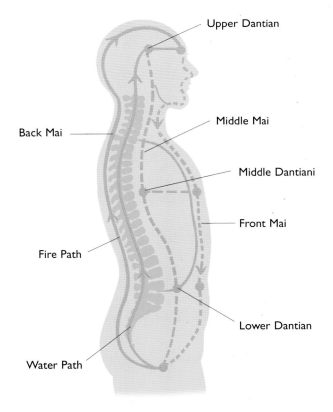

Front Mai, Back Mai and Middle Mai, including the Fire Path, and Water Path

Dantian

The extraordinary vessels (mai), especially the front mai and back mai, are reservoirs of qi. However, there are areas within the head and torso that are pierced centrally by the middle mai and intersect with the front mai and back mai. These have especially abundant qi, and are collectively known as 'dantian' or 'seas of qi'. Dantian literally translates as 'elixir field', so named because the quality and level of qi that resides within these areas is considered to be the key to a long and healthy life. The elixir fields can therefore be thought of as oceans that supply the reservoirs. The purpose of longevity meditation is to add more qi to these elixir fields so that you can have a virtually unlimited resource of energy for the purpose of extending your life as the most vibrant person

possible in order to achieve your highest goals.

By far the most important of the three dantian is the lower dantian. The front 'shore' of this sea or field is situated about 4cm/1½in below your umbilicus and is about 4cm/1½in deep. Remember that dantian is a sea of qi, so you should not think of it as just a small point in the body. However, the epicentre of this lower sea is the centre of your energy from a number of perspectives, as will become clear as you read on. For now, remember it as that area where you focus your mind whenever you want to centre your thoughts, emotions and postural balance. It is also the point from which all efficient movements are rooted and pivot around.

The other two dantian are the middle dantian, situated within the centre of your chest, and the upper dantian, situated in the region of your forehead, within the frontal lobes of your brain.

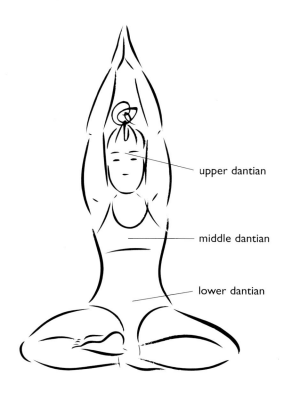

upper dantian

middle dantian

lower dantian

Energy points or 'qi vortices' along the qi channels

At specific locations along the qi channels there are gateways or cavities where qi can open to the surface. These cavities are essentially points where qi can:

- enter the channel from outside the body
- leave the channel to connect with the outside world
- represent distortions in the channel flow so that, when activated (for example by pressure, needles, or in the case of longevity meditations, by focusing the mind with unwavering attention upon them), they can affect the channel and therefore affect specific aspects of our body/mind function.

Some cavities do all of the above, while others do just two or three of them. A cavity is a vortex of qi that, if you could see it, would look like a vase-shaped swirl of energy with a mouth leading into a narrower neck, widening into a broader belly. The word 'cavity' suggests a rather dead space, but these vortices are very much alive. For that reason, I prefer to call it them 'qi vortices'.

Each of the primary channels of qi has a number of 'fixed' qi vortices. Centuries of documented observation has resulted in each qi vortex being given a name, number and recognized action on the body and mind when stimulated, either through physical pressure or mental focus.

In addition to the fixed qi vortices, there are 'transient' qi vortices, which come and go along the channels between the fixed qi vortices. Hence, due to their impermanence, they have no names or numbers. They arise where and when they do because there is either a lack of qi or an excessive build-up of qi at that location and at that point in time along the channel. Bodywork systems such as shiatsu specifically focus on rebalancing these transient qi vortices. Regular meditation practice will also naturally smooth the flow of qi throughout your body and so discourage extremes or depletions of qi at those points.

YIN-YANG

To understand further how qi behaves, it is important to have a basic understanding of yin-yang theory. Yin-yang theory is an ancient Chinese conceptual framework within the Daoist philosophy that serves as a means for viewing and understanding the world. It is the foundation for understanding all phenomena.

Imagine the Dao as the latent universe before it has manifested itself: a sort of total integration that is all-encompassing, so there is nothing with which to compare and contrast it and it cannot be perceived with our senses. Yin-yang is the duality that manifests itself out of the Dao. In other words, it polarizes the universe (Dao) into opposing phenomena that we can perceive. For example, we could not perceive light if we had no experience and concept of darkness, and vice versa. Likewise, could not grasp the idea of up if we had no concept of down. In other words, yin and yang are inseparable from the Dao, yet they are the two hands through which the Dao manifests and orders creation.

Earlier in this book, when discussing the classical Indian cosmological view, I said: "The latency of shakti is disturbed by a great cosmic vibration that splits shakti into two polarized forces known as nada and bindu. Together, these two forces become the substratum of the cosmos, providing the magnetic force to hold the molecules of the physical world together, yet in a state of vibration." If you compare this statement with the preceding paragraph, you will see that the ancient Indians and Chinese viewed the order of the cosmos in much the same way.

In Daoist terminology, the ultimate aim of those who practice meditation as a tool to gain spiritual insight is to shift their awareness beyond the everyday, familiar duality of yin-yang, to reach a perception of 'emptiness', or the state of neutrality before or between yin-yang. This state is called wuji. When you experience wuji, you experience a universe where there is no subject or object, just a continuum where everything is part of everything else. Wuji is symbolized as an empty circle. The ultimate meditator is able to move his or her perception between the reality of duality (yin-yang) and of 'no extremes' (wuji) at will.

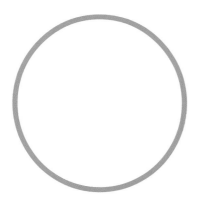

Yin-yang theory was developed during the Yin and Chou dynasties, between 1500 and 221BCE. The first mention of them in a text is in the *Yi Jing* (or I Ching), the *Book of Changes*, in around 800 BCE and it is the aspect of change and of process that is at the heart of yin-yang theory.

The original image given to reflect the respective qualities of yin and yang was of two sides of a hill. Yin is the cloudy or shady side of the hill and yang is the sunny side. On the yang side it is light, warm and people are working, while on the yin side it is cold, shady and everyone is resting.

Seen in this way, yin and yang are opposing qualities:

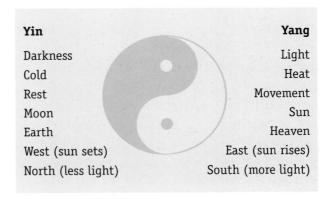

Yin	Yang
Darkness	Light
Cold	Heat
Rest	Movement
Moon	Sun
Earth	Heaven
West (sun sets)	East (sun rises)
North (less light)	South (more light)

Yin and Yang are not simply phenomena sorted into fixed categories, however. They are a way of explaining dynamic processes. Yin and yang are relative terms. Something is yin (or yang) only in relation to something else. So a 100-watt light bulb is more yang than a 30-watt bulb, but it is more yin than the sun. So to say that an apple, for instance, is yin, would be incorrect. It may be yin (colder) in relation to a steaming bowl of soup, or it may be yang (warmer) in relation to a tub of ice cream. It does not make sense to talk of yin except in relation to yang; they are opposing but also complementary. The two make up the full picture, and without the one the other is incomplete. The taiji symbol, the symbol of yin-yang, consists of two main parts, one light and one dark (most often depicted as one black and one white).

Yang is the white part of the symbol and yin is the black part. The two components coil around each other, they penetrate each other, they fade into one another. They are opposites yet they complement one another. The white part of the symbol contains a black spot and the black part a white spot, showing that nothing is ever entirely yin or yang but each contains something of the other, which may grow so that eventually each can become its opposite.

Yin and yang phenomena can themselves be further divided into yin and yang. For example, day is yang compared to night, but a day may be divided into morning and afternoon. Morning, when the sun is rising, is more yang than the afternoon, when the sun is setting, so morning is yang and afternoon is yin. Morning turns into afternoon, and in the same way yang turns into yin, and yin into yang. Day becomes night, summer turns to winter, our bodies move then rest, we are warm then cool, we wake and then sleep. The movement from yin to yang is therefore cyclical.

Another way of looking at yin and yang is to regard them as different states or stages of being. In the course of the cyclical movement from yang to yin and back again, matter takes on different forms. It is transformed. For example, day turns to night and during the day the sun evaporates water from the earth and seas, forming vapour that condenses as evening approaches and is precipitated as dew during the cool of the night. That which evaporates, rises and is less substantial or formless is yang in relation to that which condenses, falls downwards, is substantial and has form, which is yin. To take this a little further, that which is non-material, more refined, less tangible and energetic rather than solid is yang in relation to what is solid, material and tangible, which is yin. Returning to the yin-yang categories of earlier, and remembering that these are relative qualities, we can add to the list as follows:

Yin	Yang
Matter/substance	Energy/thought
Solid/liquid	Vapour/gas
Condensation	Evaporation
Contraction	Expansion
Descending	Rising
Below	Above
Form	Activity
Water	Fire
Yielding	Resistant
Soft	Hard
Passive	Aggressive
Introverted	Outgoing
Quiet	Loud
Slow	Fast
Wet	Dry
Chronic	Acute

There is a lot more to yin and yang, but the above list should give a general idea of the nature of yin-yang.

NEI DAN THEORY AND
METHODOLOGY

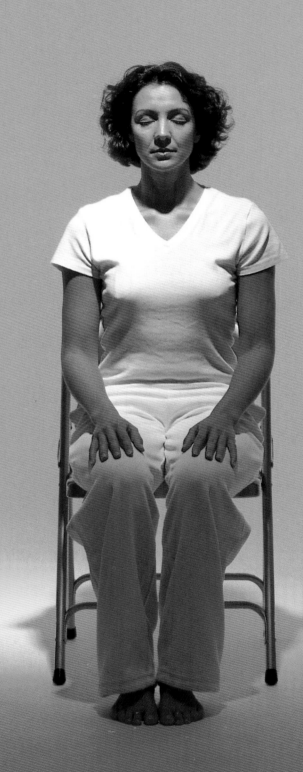

Daoist meditations for longevity and for enlightenment are referred to as 'internal elixir' methods (nei dan). Traditionally they have been kept hidden and taught only to select disciples within closed circles. This is because the nei dan methods are considered difficult to understand, dangerous to practitioners if they get them wrong, and require very close personal supervision to recognize the correct sensations that mark progress. The deepest levels of nei dan practice require a level of time and restraint that few people are able to give or achieve. They require a high degree of sexual abstinence to conserve one's essence (jing) and freedom from distraction to practice full time.

However, some of the elementary and less intense methods of nei dan for health and longevity can be practiced within everyday life, although only a certain level of achievement can be reached this way. Some elementary examples are given in this book and these levels of achievement are well worth the effort for those willing to learn them correctly and with patience. Theories pertaining to nei dan are explained in some books dealing specifically with nei dan practice. Some of these are listed in the bibliography given at the end of this book (see page 215). If you want to practice the deeper nei dan methods, you will need to find a suitable and qualified teacher first. Unfortunately, there are not many qualified teachers around, especially those who have the time to teach others, given that serious nei dan practice is more or less a full-time occupation in itself.

Nei dan for longevity can be divided into passive and active methods. Passive nei dan methods are meditative practices that emphasize stillness, awareness of internal movements and 'attitudes' of qi, plus some internal visualizations. These can be done while sitting, lying or standing. Active methods emphasize slow movement, normally in a standing position, with or without specific methods of breathing. Active methods do not include the very deep nei dan practices, but are an excellent way of learning to connect with your qi.

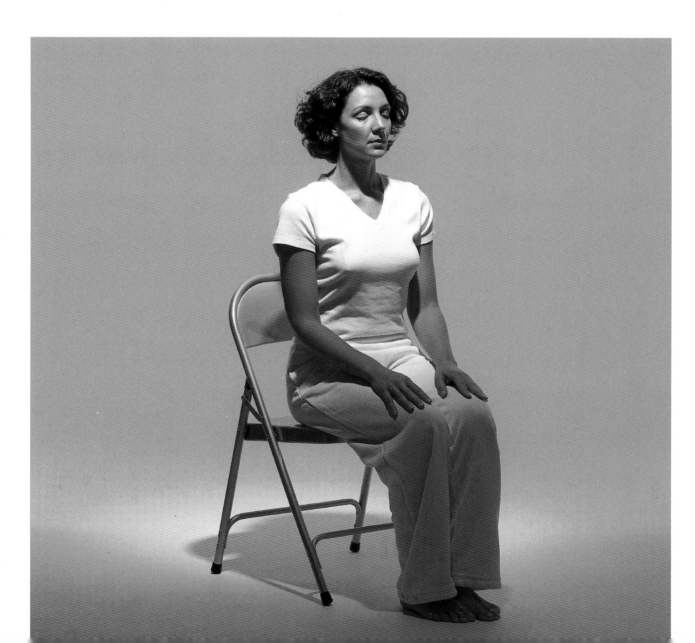

Nei dan preparatory practices are employed to open up the 'small circulation' (xiao zhou tian), sometimes called 'lesser heavenly circuit' or 'microcosmic orbit'. This circuit is formed by the joining of the front mai and back mai.

The method for preparing the opening of the small circulation is to increase qi in the lower dantian through abdominal breathing or by simply focusing your mind on your lower abdomen. Abdominal breathing is fully explained on pages 192–195. When qi is sufficiently abundant in the lower dantian, the practitioner uses his or her mind to lead the qi down from the dantian to the perineum and then to the tip of the tailbone (coccyx). From the tip of the tailbone the qi is led up the back of the spine, over the crown of the head and down the front of the body, then back to the lower dantian to complete the cycle. This circuit is the way qi naturally circulates in a healthy person.

As a basic practice, the small circulation can be visualized (or better still, 'experienced') to encourage the natural circulation of qi gently within that circuit. It is an exercise where your mindful intention (yi) leads your qi. This in itself will result in discernible health benefits over time. A simple technique for this is given as follows, although it is best not to do it if you are pregnant or menstruating, unless under the direct guidance of an experienced teacher.

Small circulation visualization exercise

1 Place the tip of your tongue on the roof of your mouth and keep it there throughout the meditation. This creates a bridge that allows qi to circulate freely along the back mai into the front mai (see 163).

2 Adopt your preferred meditation posture and rest your mental focus on your lower belly, observing but not influencing the natural expanding and withdrawing of your belly as you breathe.

3 After a minute or two, narrow your focus down to a single point about 4cm/1½in below your navel and about 4cm/1½in deep. If you find it difficult to hold your attention there, press a finger into that spot to cause a sensation on which your mind can focus.

4 After another minute or so, focus on a line descending from that point directly towards a midpoint between your genitals and anus (perineum), then continue the line to the tip of your coccyx. If necessary, use pressure from a finger to help provide a sensation that will act as a focus. The tip of the coccyx is one of three 'gates' that must be opened to enable qi to pass through. Although there are other gates, these three gates are particularly difficult areas to lead qi through. They require particular attention because your mental focus will tend to disperse when you come to them. The three main gates are:

■ the tip of your coccyx
■ the space between your second and third lumbar vertebrae
■ on the back of your head, just above and either side of the occipital protuberance (the part that protrudes at the back of the head).

5 With your mind, feel the line run up the back of your spine from your coccyx to the mid-lumbar curve, which is the next 'gate' to dwell upon and get past. The exact point is one intervertebral space above the line connecting the highest points of the two iliac crests. Rub the spot for a few seconds to create a sensation if that helps to focus your mind. Focus on the line continuing up your spine to the back of your head. Here, the problem is that your focus may dissipate over your skull. You need to keep it running centrally along the midline. Rub either side of your occipital protuberance if you need the stimulation to draw your mind to the area. Focus there for a minute or so.

6 Once past the occipital gate, carefully guide your mind over the midline of your skull, to the spot between your eyebrows (or just above). Then, without much delay, lead your attention down to the tip of your tongue. Swallow, and use the descent of your saliva as an image to lead your mind centrally down behind your breast-bone and down the mid-line of your torso back into the lower dantian.

7 Continue leading qi around this circuit for as long as you can do so comfortably. Thirty-six circuits is a traditional number to aim for, but build up to that with patience. If you start to lose focus, rub the part of the line or the gate you are trying to visualize.

8 When you have finished, place your hands on your lower dantian and simply observe your breathing (without influencing it) for two or three minutes. Then place your right fist on your navel and circle it 36 times in a clockwise direction if you are a man (that is, up the right side of your belly and down the left side), or 36 times anti-clockwise if you are a woman. With each rotation, allow the circle to grow slightly larger, but stay within the soft flesh of your abdomen. When you have completed 36 circles, reverse the direction for 24 circles, gradually spiraling inwards towards your navel. This will gather up and store the increased qi generated by the meditation.

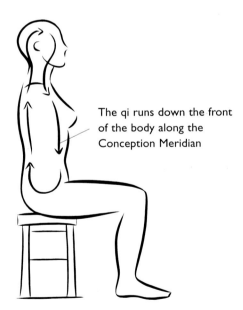

The qi runs down the front of the body along the Conception Meridian

Qi flows around the body along the meridians in an unbroken circuit, known as the small circulation of qi.

There are a number of techniques to help you get into this type of meditation. One popular method is to 'smile' your way around the circuit, visualizing an inner smile moving along the route and dissolving obstructions at the gates. If you have a visual mind, visualizing light making the journey is also useful. Visualization is not quite the same as actually feeling and experiencing, but it is a way into them.

DAOIST STANDING
MEDITAITON

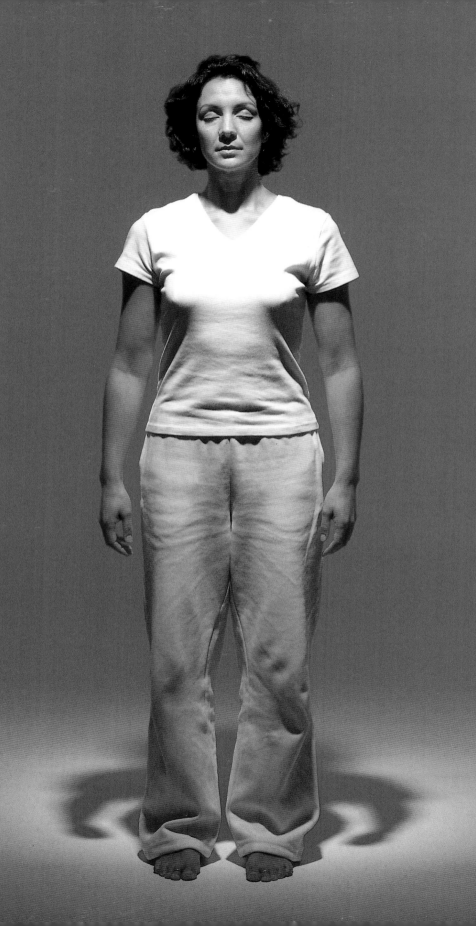

A very good practice for encouraging qi circulation is to stand mindfully. In meditative standing, the important thing is to hold your spine in vertical alignment between your pelvis and head to get maximum polarity between heaven qi and earth qi, so that maximum heaven qi and earth qi are attracted into your body. Specifically, you should make sure that the centre of your perineum, which is situated between your legs, midway between your anus and genitals, is in vertical alignment with the top of your head, on the midpoint of the line between the apex of your ears. This vertical alignment should extend down to a line level with a point on top of each foot, which lies in a depression between the two prominent tendons on the front of each ankle joint.

If you lose this vertical alignment by bending forwards, you will inhibit the ability of your lungs to inhale efficiently, thus denying yourself optimum oxygen/qi uptake from the air. If you bend backwards, you will compress your spinal joints and block the flow of qi along your spine, losing the polarity and connection between heaven qi and earth qi within your body. In fact, your spinal joints should be encouraged to 'open' as much as possible to get maximum distance between your head and pelvis, thus maintaining maximum length in your spinal column. This is because qi flows much more easily through joints that move freely and have space within them than through those that are stiff and contracted.

Paradoxically, consciously pushing your head and pelvis in opposite directions will merely contract your postural muscles and shorten your spine. Lengthening and true alignment of the spine can only be achieved through relaxation and mental focus. If you remember to check your alignment, relaxation and mental focus frequently during any of the movements and positions, you will progress steadily.

So in this basic starting position, you can benefit from reflecting upon the melding of heaven qi and earth qi within humanity, where the downward flow of heaven qi meets the upward flow of earth qi. When you are truly proficient at standing, you could incorporate the basic small circulation meditation as described earlier (see pages 176–177).

When you are in the standing position, it is best to keep your feet as near parallel to each other as possible. Here, parallel means that the big toes should be the same distance apart as the heels. If the toes are closer together than the heels, the lumbar gate will be too open, causing a loss of energy from it. If the toes are too wide in relation to the heels, the lumbar gate will remain closed, preventing qi flowing up the back mai.

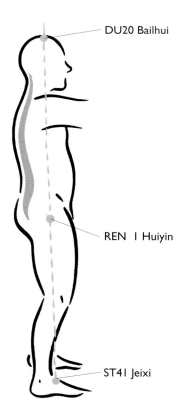

DU20 Bailhui

REN 1 Huiyin

ST41 Jeixi

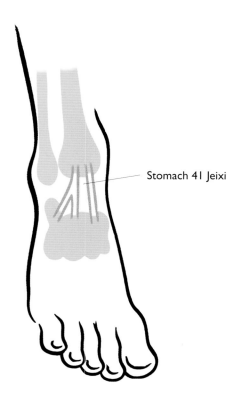

Stomach 41 Jeixi

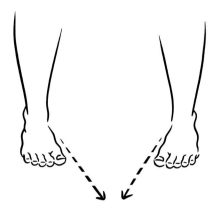

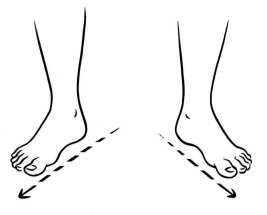

Meditative standing stance

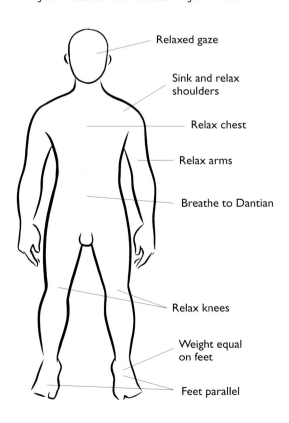

Relaxed gaze

Sink and relax shoulders

Relax chest

Relax arms

Breathe to Dantian

Relax knees

Weight equal on feet

Feet parallel

1 Stand with your feet parallel, placed between hip width and shoulder width apart or slightly wider if that is more comfortable; imagine a large ball is stopping them from drifting together. Keep your knees slightly bent – just enough to unlock them. Do not allow the knees to extend beyond the toes. Your weight should be evenly distributed between your heels and the balls of your feet.

2 If you are outside standing at a high point, fix your eyes on the horizon. If you are indoors, or with no view of a far horizon, look forward and slightly downwards. However, if you are a complete beginner, it is recommended that you keep your eyes shut during the first few weeks of practice, so that you can direct all your attention inwards without distraction. If your eyes are open, or when you do eventually open your eyes, keep them very relaxed, not wide open or closed, but somewhere in between. This is synonymous with a relaxed demeanour, where you are receptive to feeling subtle sensations and where your attention will most easily relate to the present.

3 Release all tension in your neck, allowing your chin to drop very slightly as you gently hold your throat back and lift your occiput (back of your head) from your atlas vertebra (the first cervical vertebra at the top of the spine). This will lengthen your neck by naturally lifting your head up, almost like an Edwardian gentleman raising his top hat as a gesture of courtesy.

4 Drop your shoulders and elbows so that your arms hang loosely by your side. Your shoulders should not be down and back, military style, but down and slightly forwards. This will allow your chest to relax and your belly to feel and look

more 'open'. Note that this does not mean you should collapse or depress the chest. It means you should feel the ribs softening and spreading, with a sense of opening downwards. Relax your hips and abdomen. Your spine should be in natural alignment with the top of your head.

5   Now visualize your pelvis as a bowl of water positioned between your legs and lower torso. Centrally position your 'bowl' so that it is not tilted forward or backward (imagining that you are trying not to spill any water out of the bowl).

Your coccyx (base of the spine) should naturally tilt slightly forward under your torso. This will have the effect of straightening your lumbar spine.

The effect of implementing the above instructions will be that the qi will become unlocked from your upper body and collect in your lower dantian, which is the reservoir of qi in your lower abdomen.

Refining your stance

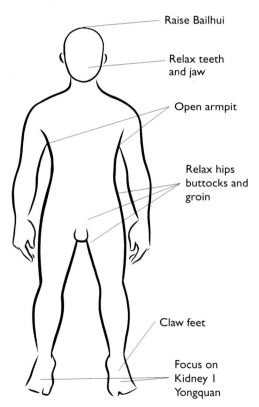

Raise Bailhui

Relax teeth and jaw

Open armpit

Relax hips buttocks and groin

Claw feet

Focus on Kidney I Yongquan

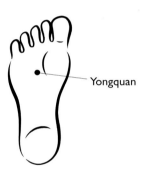

Yongquan

After a few weeks of regular practice, or when you feel ready, you can begin to include additional factors and visualizations to increase the effectiveness of your stance.

1   Focus your mind on a point just behind the centre of the balls of your feet. This point is called yongquan. Very slightly claw your feet into the ground whenever they are taking your weight. This will activate yongquan more strongly. However, if this causes tension elsewhere in your body, do not claw your feet until you gain more experience.

2   Relax and 'soften' your hips, groin, inner thighs, lower back, buttocks and belly, so that your pelvis feels like it is hanging from the centre of your dantian. Relax your teeth, jaw and shoulders. Then encourage a sense of space in your armpits. You could imagine a small ball of air in each armpit maintaining that space.

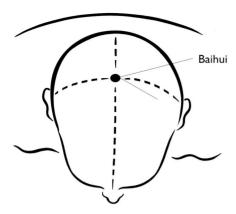

Baihui

7 While standing in this position, it is very useful to make a habit of slowly scanning your body internally from head to feet, noticing any areas of discomfort or areas that do not feel quite right. Once noticed, do not do anything with these sensations – simply be aware of them. Note that this scanning procedure is a 'feeling' exercise and not a visualizing exercise. By feeling, you will eventually acquire the ability to release your internal blockages at will.

8 Try to build up to 10 or 15 minutes per day. This will result in significant benefits to your posture within a couple of weeks. Working up to 45 minutes per day will result in significant improvements and awareness of your qi circulation, with resultant increases in vitality. However, build up slowly and surely so that you look forward to it rather than resent it. It is a lot easier to watch television, and that can seem like a more attractive option, until you start to reap some benefits.

3 Imagine you are balancing a small book on the top of your head midway between the apex of your two ears. This point is called baihui.

4 Feel your body weight relax downwards. Imagine that it is pooling and therefore filling your legs, rather like sand emptying from the top and filling the bottom half of an egg timer. Your legs should feel solid and grounded while your torso and head feel light and buoyant.

5 Within your light and buoyant torso, visualize your spinal column as a vertical pillar made of many segments. Imagine those segments drift apart slightly, so that air can circulate between those spaces. Do not will this to occur, because that will create tension, just gently imagine it. If you cannot imagine it or it does not help, just forget about it.

6 Imagine you are neck deep in water (such as a lake) wearing heavy boots that sink into the sediment on the bottom of the lake. The boots keep your feet totally grounded while your natural buoyancy within the water lengthens your vertebral column and maintains the subtle space under your armpits. All your joints will feel like they are opening, which is good because open joints enable qi to circulate more freely around your body. Your hands should be allowed to concave slightly, which will activate the centre of your palms.

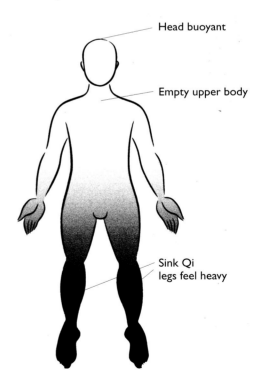

Head buoyant

Empty upper body

Sink Qi
legs feel heavy

Once you are well established in the basic
standing meditation, you could try meditating on the 'horizontal arm bow' and
'vertical spine bow'. This is an ingredient
of taiji quan practice, but is also an excellent exercise for becoming aware of how
subtle body movements integrate with the
breathing rhythm.

Neutral position   In breath

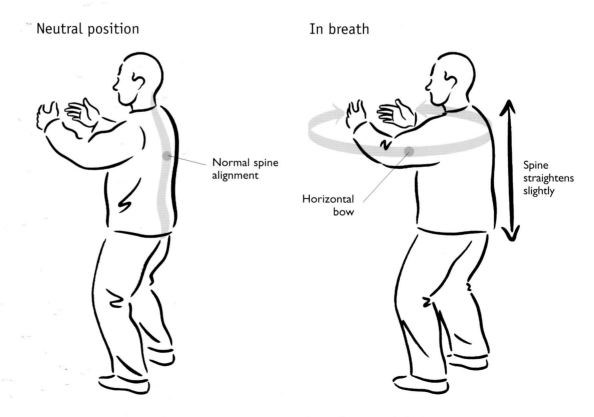

Normal spine
alignment

Horizontal
bow

Spine
straightens
slightly

Open bow on inhalation

The horizontal arm bow is a line connecting the tips of your middle fingers via the posterior (back) surface of your arms and across your upper back. The vertical spine bow is a line from your coccyx up your spine to the top of your head.

If you stand in the basic meditative standing position with your arms held relaxed and your hands in front of your torso, you will observe that as you breathe, your arms will open very slightly, causing your hands to separate a little, and your spine will straighten a fraction. This is known as 'opening the bows'. As you breathe out, your arms and hands will close a little and your spine will curve very slightly from its slight 'S' shape to a slight 'C' shape. This is referred to as 'closing the bows'. This effect is more apparent if you adopt reverse abdominal breathing (see page 195).

Out breath

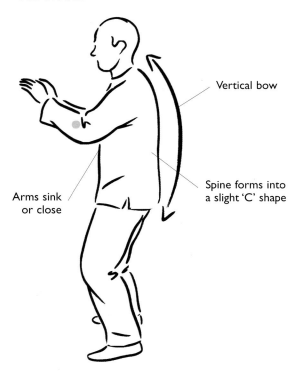

Vertical bow

Spine forms into a slight 'C' shape

Arms sink or close

Closed bow on exhalation

BREATHING METHODS FOR DAOIST MEDITATION

Some practitioners of nei dan longevity meditation like to incorporate specific patterns of breathing as an integral part of the practice. However, most prefer to ignore the breathing entirely, although only if the practitioner has established a natural pattern of breathing.

Whether or not you direct your breathing, breathing will occur regardless. So you should at least ensure that inhalation and exhalation are an unbroken continuum – one leading naturally into the other. When your breathing is especially relaxed, deep and slow, you will experience a pause at the point where inhalation changes to exhalation and exhalation changes to inhalation. However, this should not feel like a break in the continuum, but more like a point of balance as the in breath naturally transmutes into the out breath, like the stillness of dusk where day meets and yields to the night, or dawn where night meets and yields to the day.

If you feel your nostrils constrict as you inhale, it is because you are concentrating too hard on breathing rather than allowing it to manifest itself at its own strength and pace. Paradoxically, forcing the breath constricts the nostrils, so you get very little extra air for your effort. Good breathing should be soundless and cause no sensation or movement within the nostrils.

NATURAL BREATHING

It is fine simply to let your breathing happen, but you must be sure that it is happening the way it should. You need to get to the point where the breathing flows automatically, otherwise you will be splitting your attention between remembering how to breathe and trying to lead your qi, and messing up both.

Our emotions directly affect our breathing and vice versa. When we are excited, tense or angry, we breathe faster and more shallowly, and perhaps irregularly. When we are sad or depressed, we breathe in a sort of collapsed, half-measured way. When we are relaxed and at ease emotionally, we breathe more slowly, deeply and smoothly. Therefore, before you begin to practise nei dan meditation, it is important to be able to calm yourself if you are excited or motivate yourself if you are depressed. In other words, you need to regulate your emotions and thoughts. The key to this is initially to do nothing other than observe your own breathing. The very fact that you are drawing your consciousness inwards towards your breathing will begin to centre your mind. Perhaps not the first time you try it, but with repetition over time, your mind will habitually become more still (see anapana on pages 9–10). Therefore, to encourage good, natural breathing, you should do the following:

- relax
- observe and feel your breathing rather than control it
- try not to think of anything in the past or future
- breathe through your nose.

When you are truly relaxed in natural breathing, you will feel as if your breathing has its own automatic cycle, as if you are passively riding on the rhythm of your breath. If you get to the point where it feels like the air is breathing you, rather than you breathing the air, then you know you are about as relaxed and centred as it is possible to be.

Getting your breathing sorted out (or, more accurately, allowing your breathing to return to its natural rhythm) is fundamental to success in meditation. When it comes to any form of moving meditation, a good rule to remember is "meditative movement should follow the relaxed breath; the breath should never chase the movement." Adopting this rule will prevent your movements from speeding up, because if you are truly relaxed, your breathing will become slower and deeper, and your movements will follow that pace.

NORMAL ABDOMINAL BREATHING

Normal abdominal breathing is also called 'Buddhist breathing'. Most young children do this naturally, and so do some adults who have remained grounded and centred throughout the stresses of adult life, or have somehow managed to avoid heavy and repetitive stress. However, most adults find they have to relearn this method of breathing.

When you breathe in, focus on the expansion of your lower belly (dantian) as your diaphragm naturally descends. In the beginning you may need to apply conscious effort to your abdominal muscles to make this happen. When you breathe out, relax your abdomen and feel it draw in as your diaphragm ascends. If you can visualize the diaphragm doing this, that is fine. If not, just relax the belly as you fix your mind upon your dantian and it should happen naturally. Encouraging the diaphragm to move more fully in this way will help pump blood around your body and physically massage your organs. Also, because you are focusing on the dantian, energy will be concentrated there, giving you a grounded center from which vitality will manifest itself. As you inhale, it will feel like your breath is being pulled all the way down to the dantian, but of course, in reality, the air will go no lower than your diaphragm.

Once you have got your abdominal muscles doing the right thing, you should then incorporate a lift and relaxation of your perineum, specifically a point known as huiyin, situated between your anus and genitals. When you contract your belly during exhalation, you should gently pull huiyin up. When you expand your belly during inhalation you should gently encourage huiyin to descend and 'open'. In the beginning you may find that you cannot pull up or descend huiyin. Instead, when you try to do it, you may find you pull up or descend your anus. That is normal and still quite effective. After some practice you will begin to feel movement at huiyin, but accompanied by

movement of the anus. As time goes on, you will be able to increase the focus and movement at huiyin and decrease the movement of the anus. Basically, this movement is the same as a gentle pelvic floor exercise, which tends to be more familiar to women than to men. Once you are comfortably established in natural abdominal breathing, you will be able to do it automatically within your longevity meditations while your mind is focused on other specific body parts, sensations or images.

Air is drawn in slowly and evenly to the bottom of the lungs. The diaphragm is pressed down and the abdomen expanded.

Upon exhalation the abdomen is relaxed and drawn in.

Normal abdominal breathing

When inhaling the stomach is drawn in.

As air is expelled the stomach is relaxed and expanded.

Reverse abdominal breathing

REVERSE ABDOMINAL BREATHING

Reverse abdominal breathing is also called 'Daoist breathing'. In reverse abdominal breathing, you draw the abdomen in when inhaling and allow the abdomen to relax and expand when exhaling: the opposite of normal abdominal breathing. The relative pressure difference between the chest cavity and abdominal cavity produces a stronger pumping effect compared to normal breathing.

In reverse abdominal breathing, you hold up huiyin as you inhale and draw your abdomen in. You descend and 'open' huiyin as you exhale and expand your abdomen. It is recommended that this method is only used for a few breaths at a time, unless you are working directly with an experienced teacher. In all respects, reverse abdominal breathing is more powerful than normal abdominal breathing, but it can also cause more problems if too much is practiced too soon, or if it is done incorrectly. The biggest pitfall is holding the breath when really the in breath and out breath should flow seamlessly from one to the other.

One reason for doing reverse abdominal breathing rather than normal abdominal breathing is to build up the qi that circulates predominantly on the exterior of the body. This type of qi is called 'defensive qi'. It protects the body from external agents such as excessive heat or cold. Once you are established in reverse abdominal breathing, you will find that you can switch from normal to reverse breathing at any time.

DAOIST MOVING
MEDITAITONS

ॐ

TIMING THE BREATH

In the moving meditations that will be described shortly, breathing should be in time with your movements or, more accurately, your movements should follow the pace of your relaxed breathing.

In general, inhaling accompanies your 'opening' movements, and exhaling accompanies your 'closing' movements. Also, you should inhale with rising movements and exhale with sinking movements. Breathing and moving simultaneously will give you an experience of breathing with your entire body, not just with your lungs. After much practice, you will eventually have the sensation that the breath is entering through your skin. Some of it does anyway, but you will begin to appreciate this at an experiential level. At this stage, your moving meditation will be giving you a real connection to your environment.

As stated earlier, the most important thing to remember about breathing is that the movements should follow the breath; the breath should not chase the movements. In other words, only move in time with your relaxed inward and outward breath. Thus, the more relaxed your breathing, the slower your movements will be. Impatience will cause you to rush through the movements to get them over, causing your breathing to speed up. Constantly check yourself for this, because when that happens you are completely wasting your time.

Do the following moving meditations for as long as you want. You may find that, when you get going, you will not want to stop. That is fine. Just keep going if you have time.

Moving meditation 1: Connecting to the earth

1 Stand naturally with your arms relaxed by your side, feet parallel, about shoulder-width apart, and your knees very slightly bent. Look directly ahead or very slightly down, with your eyelids open but relaxed. Allow your eyelids to close if you are facing directly into the rising or setting sun.

2 Before you begin to move, fix your mind on your lower belly (dantian) for two or three breaths. As you inhale, raise your arms forwards in front of you with palms down, to slightly higher than shoulder height. Bend your knees slightly as

you do this, but ensure your knees do not project beyond your toes.

3 As you exhale, allow your hands to sink down gradually to waist height. Straighten your knees slightly as you do so. Your back should be straight but relaxed throughout. Your elbows should be unlocked and your relaxed fingers will naturally curl slightly. If you find it difficult to keep your neck relaxed and upright, visualize something light in weight balancing on your head throughout the movement.

Note: the knees bend when the arms are raised because in this exercise we want to establish a clear awareness of heaven qi moving through our body from above to below. Qi moving predominantly in this direction, rather than upwards through the body, is necessary for general well-being. In other words, we need to establish a strong sense of 'grounding'. To exaggerate this effect, try raising your hands quickly. You should feel a sudden heaviness in your buttocks and feet as you do so. Experiential feelings such as this are difficult to convey in words. Experiment and play with this movement a little and meditate on the nuances for yourself.

Adding imagery

The terms 'visualize' and 'imagery' refer to clues as to what you may eventually feel. Most people have better powers of visual imagery compared to their sense of feeling/sensing qi. However, with practice you will definitely develop the ability to feel as well as, or instead of, to visualize.

■ As you lower your arms, imagine that your feet are sinking far into the ground. Then, when you raise your arms forwards in front of you, feel your qi descending from your lower dantian into the ground to meet with the earth deep underground.

■ This is useful if you are feeling 'full' and 'blocked' and want to dissolve or transform the feeling. As you raise your arms and inhale, imagine clear water (if you feel hot) or warm fine sand (if you feel cold) being sucked up through the soles of your feet into your legs and filling your entire body, absorbing and transforming the tensions, stress, pain, anger or whichever feelings you want to transform. As you lower your arms and exhale, feel the water or sand flood out through the soles of your feet and descend deep into the earth to be replaced with fresh water or sand during your next inhalation.

■ If you are feeling 'empty' and listless and want to absorb fresh qi from your surroundings, imagine you are enveloped within a ball of pure white light or fluid-like nectar which you absorb as you do the movements.

Moving meditation 2: Standing your ground to absorb the sea

Moving meditations where one foot is placed in front of the other, and the weight rocks forwards and backwards to transfer weight between the feet, lend themselves particularly well to a strong feeling of deep connection into the ground.

1 Stand with one leg in front of the other. When you lean forwards, you should raise your back heel. When you lean backwards, you should raise your front toes by balancing on the heel.

2 Take your weight on your back foot. As you inhale, raise your arms forwards to shoulder height, palms down. Bring your hands back towards your chest.

3 As you exhale, shift your weight to your front foot, straightening your back leg and bending your front leg as you extend your arms forwards, palms facing the front, as if you are pushing the waves away.

4 Inhale again as you lean into your back foot and bring your hands back towards your chest, palms down. The cycle then repeats itself as you again exhale and extend your arms. Keep your spine, head and neck in vertical alignment throughout.

Adding imagery

■ Imagine you are pulling the sea towards you when you inhale and pull back your arms. Imagine you are pushing the sea away from you as you exhale and extend your arms forwards.

■ As you pull the sea towards you, feel yourself firmly standing your ground as the wave washes through you, loosening, cooling and transforming your tensions and anxieties, or, if you prefer, dragging tensions and anxieties out through the back of your body.

■ As you push your arms forward, imagine the wave that passed through you returns through your back and completes the cooling and transforming process, or, if you prefer, washes out more tension through the front of your body.

■ After a few repetitions you could switch your intention to absorbing the power of the sea as you draw it in and push it out. You could imagine that wave power is charging up your kidneys rather like a wave-powered hydroelectricity generator.

■ If you also feel your feet extending down deep into the ground as each one in turn takes the weight, this exercise becomes even more effective because it adds to the sense of 'standing your ground.'

■ The imagery of absorbing the latent power of the ocean is very strong in this exercise. The power of the ocean represents the most powerful energy on the planet, which is even able to erode continents. Once it is on the move (tidal movement) nothing can stop it. Hence, this meditation is excellent for increasing your will power.

■ When you lower your hands to your belly, palms downwards, as you exhale, draw your attention from your nose, down the midline of your body to the tailbone.

■ When you raise your hands, turning your palms towards you as you inhale, draw your attention from the tailbone to the nose, then continue with another circuit during the next breath and so on. This works particularly well if you adopt reverse abdominal breathing (see page 195).

Note: It is good to end this exercise by just resting your palms on your lower belly for a few moments, either standing or sitting. This acts to 'close you down' a little, because, while performing the exercises, your energy will have opened up to the subtleties of surrounding qi. You could also circle your fists into your belly.

Moving meditation 3: Balancing qi

This moving meditation is a good one to practice if you want to focus on the small circulation (see pages 175–177).

1 Stand in the basic standing meditation position with your palms in front of your lower belly, fingers pointing at each other.
2 As you inhale, lift your hands to eye level, allowing the palms to turn towards you slightly.

3 As you exhale, turn your palms downwards and allow your hands to sink down towards your belly. Allow your knees to bend a little as you do so.

Variation: Extend your hands forwards and up, then backwards and down in a circle, rather like using the edge of your little fingers to trace the front and back of a large ball situated in front of your torso.

THE EFFECTS OF DAOIST
MEDITATION

STRENGTHENING THE EARTH ELEMENT

Beyond developing awareness of the moment that is 'now', a further benefit common to the standing and moving health and longevity meditations is the strengthening of what can be called the 'earth element' within us. Having discussed earth qi (see page 152), we can consider the earth element to be the qualities of earth qi we hold within ourselves. These qualities can all be summed up as aspects of support. The concept of support in relation to the earth becomes clear when we consider how the earth literally supports us by providing the ground upon which we stand, our shelter and the food we eat. It is the centre of our existence in every way.

When the qualities of planet earth are strong within us; in other words, when we have a strong earth element, we exhibit certain qualities. We have a strong feeling of being supported and of being able to support others. In a woman, a literal example of this is being able to provide milk for her newborn baby. To the baby she is the center, providing care and nourishment on all levels. If our earth element is

weak, we might feel like nobody is supporting our needs and we are thus too insecure to support others.

Strong earth qi within us will also enable us to assimilate the essence of the earth, which to us is food. Hence, a robust digestive system indicates that our earth qi is strong. If our earth element is weak, we can develop digestive problems and undernourishment based on the inability to assimilate enough essential nutrients.

For us, the gravity and solidity of planet earth holds everything together. Therefore, our ability to hold ourselves together physically is evident by the tone of our flesh and the fact that our connective tissues support our vital organs. If our earth element is weak, the tone of our muscles and connective tissues may weaken, causing a general sagging of the body, which at worst may lead to such things as varicose veins or the prolapse of certain organs.

It is because we have the ground to stand upon that we have a familiar base or point of reference from which to look up at the heavens. The solidity

of the earth enables us to recognize the comparative 'emptiness' of the sky, and so a solid feeling of being grounded enables us to open up to the vibrations of the heavens. This means that because earth qi enters us, mostly through our feet, we are able to open up to heaven qi, which enters mostly through our head. This is similar to a plant rooting itself into the ground so that it can reach up to the sunlight, which is the plant's most important form of heaven qi. If our earth element is weak, we could have trouble with physical balance, much like a plant with shallow roots. Also, the lack of a stable base will prevent us from having the polarity to connect with the more subtle aspects of heaven qi, such as intuition.

In practice this means that, by being more grounded, through the practice of the meditations previously described, we will naturally cause a greater downward movement of heaven qi through our bodies. This is important to understand, because a fundamental principle of Daoist longevity meditation is that the unimpeded flow of heaven qi moving down and through us from above is a key factor in maintaining both physical health and emotional stability. Being grounded in reality or, to use a very apt expression, 'having our feet firmly on the ground', gives us a stable base from which to perceive things clearly. This is in contrast to those who are not grounded, who are often referred to as 'spaced out'. Thus, the ability to perceive and think clearly is largely dependent upon being well connected to earth qi, which in turn anchors our mind and enables us to use our thinking abilities (our yi, which can then lead our qi). Consequently, if our earth element is weak, our thinking process will be confused rather than lucid. For one thing, this will make the ability to focus our mind within meditation very difficult.

In brief then, most standing or moving longevity meditations, by virtue of the great emphasis placed upon having a firmly rooted stance, draw abundant earth qi into our body, which strengthens our earth element. The polarity caused by being 'earthed' through the feet creates sufficient polarity between earth and sky and space to attract heaven qi through the head (although both earth qi and heaven qi are also slightly absorbed through other parts of the body). The benefits of this are better digestion, clearer thinking, better visceral and muscular tone, stronger polarity between heaven qi and earth qi causing greater uptake of these energies, a deeper sense of feeling supported and a greater capacity to give support to others.

The other universal benefit of all moving longevity meditations is a smoother flow and distribution of qi and blood. This is because the movements of the exercises have a fluid, wavelike quality that gently stimulates the circulation of blood, particularly through the joints, thus helping to lubricate them. A smoother flow of qi also impacts on our mind, causing a greater equanimity of emotion.

If you add all those things together and get them right, you should feel pretty good. However, it is worth remembering the meaning of this little maxim: **"Reading about it might make you do it, but doing it makes it happen!"**

Motivation

Sometimes you will not want to do these qigong exercises, or you will start off, but be totally uninspired to continue. For some people this happens very occasionally, while for others it happens most of the time. You will probably fall somewhere in between. Usually it goes in phases, so you might go for periods of time where you cannot wait to start and do not want to stop.

Other phases will include periods of total ambivalence or inertia. This is quite normal, and it helps to know that you are not the only one who experiences these swings in motivation. Just persevere, and you will soon reap the benefits that the continued practice of meditation can bring.

Possible side effects

The effects of doing longevity meditation are overwhelmingly positive. You will have more energy, better concentration, increased equanimity of mind and emotional stability, improved posture and flexibility, greater endurance, better digestion, greater body awareness, greater appreciation of your personal space and of your surroundings, more awareness of other people's space and an enhanced intuitive insight.

You may or may not experience some mild reactions from time to time, but these are also ultimately positive because they either reflect some sort of cleansing reaction, or they indicate a problem with your practice which you can then correct. Reactions that are physical sensations usually happen while you are practicing or shortly after. However, you are unlikely to experience these reactions to any degree unless you are doing a lot of focused and intense meditation.

The most common side effects are itching and pain in various parts of the body. This can indicate an area of your body where the qi is unable to get through, thus causing an accumulation or 'fulness' in that area. These side effects are very useful, because they highlight a specific area on which to focus. They are very commonly felt in the shoulders, back, neck and arms. The solution is to 'open' the joints of the fingers, hands, wrists, elbows and shoulders. The best way to do that is to keep practicing the standing and moving meditations until such sensations dissolve and transform. Doing so will also add to your understanding of impermanence.

Some people experience flatulence or diarrhoea for a short time. This can be a natural cleansing reaction as your body strengthens and rebalances itself through the movement of qi. Excessive salivation may occur, but this can be a natural cleansing reaction as your body strengthens and rebalances itself through the movement of qi.

Another possible occurrence is the manifestation of spontaneous movement as you meditate. You are very unlikely to experience this within the meditations described in this book, but if you do it will only happen if your mind is relaxed, 'empty' and dwelling in the present. It is therefore a good sign. True spontaneous movement will be experienced as originating from your lower dantian. It represents the radical shifting of blocked qi.

The concept of distorted qi

In Daoist longevity meditation, there are two slightly opposing views as to the nature of discomfort and the resolution of it. One idea is that all forms of discomfort, whether physical or emotional, ultimately represent distorted qi, which must be dissolved or transformed into free-flowing qi before the discomfort will subside. Another view is that this distorted qi is better expelled than transformed. Within the latter view, this distorted qi is referred to as negative qi or sick qi. In reality, it is likely that elements of both views hold true.

Distorted qi can also refer to negative attitudes of mind, especially repressed or stuck emotions. For example, if you hold the image of flushing out or 'letting go' of stored anger or envy, you are in a way, expelling negative qi. By contrast, the 'transforming' viewpoint prefers the image of allowing the emotion to dissolve or transform simply by being mindfully aware of its existence. The enhanced qi circulation acquired through longevity meditation will naturally transform this blocked energy (which is what all pain and repressed or stuck emotions represent) into free-flowing energy.

The 'transforming' viewpoint has two sub-viewpoints within it, especially in relation to stuck emotions. One view is as just described, that recognizing the problem will unlock it, enabling the meditative process to transform and move it naturally. The other view is that an unwanted emotional state is best transformed by supplanting it with the opposite feeling or attitude. For example, if you feel angry, imagine that you are surrounded by a halo of joy.

Of course, problems in the body, such as physical pain, can initiate negative mental attitudes, and repressed emotions can lead to physical problems, so there is not always a clear distinction between these problems. Either way, mindfully observing these 'problems' ultimately shows them to be impermanent, although that means they may simply change into something else equally unsatisfactory, rather than disappear altogether. However, meditation should help you cope with the 'unsatisfactory' more easily, and sometimes dissolve current problematic issues altogether.

A CLOSING WORD OR SO

A lot of detailed 'technical' information has been given in this book. Hopefully this will have given you a broad understanding of some traditional eastern meditation methods.

My aim in writing this book was to stimulate some interest for the beginner in meditation, and also to introduce some useful concepts to the more experienced meditator. Those who base their meditation practice on an Indian system should, from this book, clearly see the parallels and differences with the Daoist system, and vice versa. This surely reflects the parallels and differences between these cultures. Also, the fact that the roots of these methods have existed at least since the dawn of recorded history suggests that the need for some sort of investigative and practical spiritual quest seems to be part of the human condition.

Some people may argue that science is the new tool for understanding reality, but modern physics is actually not so far removed from many Buddhist, yogic or Daoist teachings. Perhaps then, it is not a question of ancient versus modern, but of new embracing old.

There is a wealth of written information available on all forms of meditation, spiritual practice and science in relation to meditation and ancient philosophies. The bibliography (opposite) represents a doorway into this vast arena of information.

Theos Bernard, *Hatha Yoga*
  Rider & Company, London 1950
Alexander Berzin, *Developing Balanced Sensitivity*
  Snow Lion Publications, New York 1998
Buddhadasa Bhikku, *Heartwood of the Bodhi Tree*
  Wisdom Publications, Boston 1994
Buddhadasa Bhikku, *Mindfulness with Breathing*
  Wisdom Publications, Boston 1988
Dalai Lama X14, *Beyond Dogma*
  Souvenir Press, London 1996
Dalai Lama X14, *Cultivating a Daily Meditation*
  Library of Tibetan Works and Archives, Dharamsala 1991
Dalai Lama X14, *The Good Heart*
  Rider, London 1997
Dalai Lama X14, *Kindness, Clarity and Insight*
  Snow Lion Publications, New York 1984
Dalai Lama X14, *Path to Bliss*
  Snow Lion Publications, New York 1991
Dalai Lama X14, *Selected Works of the Dalai Lama 111*
  Snow Lion Publications, New York 1983
Swami Vishnu Devananda, *Meditation and Mantras*
  OM Lotus Publishing Company, New York 1981
Sandy Eastoak, *Dharma Family Treasures*
  North Atlantic Books, Berkeley 1994
Fremantle & Trungpa, *The Tibetan Book of the Dead*
  Shambala Publications, Boston 1975
Fontana & Slack, *Teaching Meditation to Children*
  Element Books, Shaftesbury 1997
Je Gampopa, *Gems of Dharma, Jewels of Freedom*
  Translated by Ken & Katia Holmes, Altea Publishing, Forres,
  Scotland 1995
Joseph Goldstein, *Insight Meditation*
  Shambala Publications, Boston 1993
Daniel Goleman, *Healing Emotions*
  Shambala Publications, Boston 1997
Lama Anagarika Govinda, *Foundations of Tibetan Mysticism*
  Rider, London 1960
Bede Griffiths, *Return to the Centre*
  Collins, Glasgow 1976
Ven. Lobsang Gyatso, *The Four Noble Truths*
  Snow Lion Publications, New York 1994
Thich Nhat Hanh, *Touching Peace*
  Parallax Press, Berkeley California 1992
James Hewitt, *Teach Yourself Yoga*, Third Edition
  Hodder & Stoughton, London 1988
Jeffrey Hopkins, *The Tantric Distinction*
  Wisdom Publications, Boston 1984
BKS Iyengar, *Light on Yoga*
  George Allen & Unwin, London 1966
Alan James, *The Unfolding of Wisdom*
  Aukana, Bradford on Avon, 1994
Chris Jarmey, *Taiji Qigong*
  Corpus publishing, Winchester 2001

Kalu Rinpoche, *Gently Whispered*
  Station Hill Press, New York 1994
Jonathan Landaw and Andy Weber, *Images of Enlightenment,
  Tibetan Art in Practice*
  Snow Lion Publications, New York 1993
Kathleen MacDonald, *How to Meditate, a Practical Guide*
  Wisdom Publications, London 1984
Ian Macwhinnie, *The Radiant Kingdom*
  Benwell Books, Rugby 1994
Pabongka Rinpoche, *Liberation in the Palm of Your Hand*
  Wisdom Publications, Boston 1991
Patrul Rinpoche, *The Words of My Perfect Teacher*
  Altamira Press, Walnut Creek, California 1994
Sayadaw U Pandita, *In This Very Life*
  Wisdom Publications, Boston 1992
Penguin Classics, *The Upanishads*
  Penguin Books, Middx 1965
John Powers, *Introduction to Tibetan Buddhism*
  Snow Lion Publications, New York 1995
Geshe's Rabten and Dhargyey, *Advice from a Spiritual Friend*
  Wisdom Publications, London 1984
Geshe Rabten, *Practical Meditation*
  Tharpa Choeling, Hamburg 1981
Geshe Sonam Rinchen, *The 37 Practices of Bodhisattvas*
  Snow Lion Publications, New York 1997
Shantideva, *A Guide to the Bodhisattva's Way of Life*
  Library of Tibetan Works and Archives, Dharamsala 1979
  Snow Lion Publications, New York 1997
Ajahn Sumedho, *The Mind and The Way*
  Rider, London 1996
Tarthang Tulku, *Skillful Means*
  Dharma Publishing, Oakland 1978
Saya U Chit Tin & Roger Bischoff, *Dhamma Texts Series 1 to 14*
  International Meditation Centres, Heddington, Wiltshire
  1982, 1987 and 1992
Saya U Chit Tin, *The Perfection of Virtue*
  The Sayagi U Ba Khin Memorial Trust, UK, Heddington,
  Wiltshire 1987
Christopher Titmuss, *The Green Buddha*
  Insight Books, Totnes 1995
Tsong-kha-Pa, *The Great Treatise on the Stages of the Path
  to Enlightenment*
  (Lam Rim Chen Mo)
  Snow Lion Publications, New York 2000
Chogyam Trungpa, *The Myth of Freedom*
  Shambala Publications, Boston & London 1988
Dr. Yang, Jwing-Ming, *The Root of Chinese Qigong*
  YMAA Publication Center, Massachusetts 1989
Geshe Wangyal, *The Jewelled Staircase*
  Snow Lion Publications, New York 1986
Lama Yeshe, *Introduction to Tantra*
  Wisdom Publications, Boston 1987
Lama Zopa Rinpoche, *Transforming Problems into Happiness*
  Wisdom Publications, Boston 1993

INDEX